Words, Words, Words

Words, Words, Words

HOUGHMAGANDIE, KNOCKERS,
TROLLEYS & OTHERS

Diarmaid Ó Muirithe

THE LILLIPUT PRESS
DUBLIN

First published 2004 by
THE LILLIPUT PRESS
62–63 Sitric Road, Arbour Hill,
Dublin 7, Ireland
www.lilliputpress.ie

Copyright © Diarmaid Ó Muirithe, 2004

These articles are reproduced from *The Oldie*,
by kind permission of the editor.

Cartoons by Jim Cogan
Design by Susan Waine

All rights reserved. No part of this publication may
be reproduced in any form or by any means
without the prior permission of the publisher.

A CIP record for this title is available from
The British Library.

1 3 5 7 9 10 8 6 4 2

ISBN 1 84351 059 6

The Lilliput Press receives financial assistance from
An Chomhairle Ealaíon / The Arts Council of Ireland.

Set in 11 on 14 pt Dante
Printed by ßetaprint, Bluebell, Dublin

For Brendan Kennelly
'Words alone are certain good.'

A Note from The Oldie

In the December 1996 issue of *The Oldie* we printed, as usual, a list of books published that year recommended by various contributors to the magazine. I am used to fairly obscure books being nominated so was not surprised when the distinguished Irish writer William Trevor described as 'delightful' a book about the origin of words by Diarmaid Ó Muirithe, a regular contributor to the *Irish Times*.

What was surprising was the reaction of readers when given an opportunity to buy the book. Orders flooded in and we sold far and away more copies than any of the other recommendations. Encouraged by the response, I wrote to Diarmaid Ó Muirithe, offering him a regular column in the magazine. I was delighted when he accepted and he has been with us ever since.

RICHARD INGRAMS
October 2004

JANUARY 1998

CORNWALL IS ONE of my favourite places and its fishermen I got to know long before I first set foot there thirty years ago. They used to put into Kilmore Quay on the south coast of Wexford in rough weather and I remember being amused by their tales of the supernatural, many of which resembled strange stories I had previously heard around the fires of home. Their taboo words were strange to me, but for most of them we had our counterparts.

The word church, they told me, was never used on board a trawler; to do so would bring bad luck on the fishing, so they had another word for it – *cleeta*. An ancient Wexford mariner told me that his word was *clig*. I assumed that this was the Irish *clog*, a bell; the church in Kilmore Quay had neither tower nor steeple but it had a bell perched above the roof, facing the Atlantic. The Cornishmen's cleeta is from Cornish *cleghty*, a belfry; related to the Welsh *clochdy* and indeed to Irish *cloigtheach*, a bell-house. Robert Morton Nance's researches have shown that Scottish fishermen use that very term, bell-house, instead of 'kirk' while at sea, and that in Lapland it is believed that no fish can be caught anywhere in sight of a church. Steeple, tower and town are other names for the taboo church in Cornwall.

Why the words priest and minister are taboo among fishermen has long intrigued folklorists. In Orkney and Shetland men of the cloth were called *prestingolva*, *hoyden* and *upstander*, according to that treasure of a book, Ferguson's *Rambles* (1884); in northern Scotland *black coat* and *black frock*; in Donegal, *fear dubh* or *black man* is still heard; and the Irish folklorist, Bairbre O'Flynn, has heard *capishroch* along the south coast of our island: a deliberate warping of *Caipisíneach*, Capuchin friar. In Cornwall the taboo word became *white choker*. Whatever the reason, priests of all denominations are *personae non gratae* around boats. An old fisherman friend of mine, now well into his eighties, refused to attend the blessing of a new lifeboat by the Catholic and Anglican priests of his village. No luck would come of it, he said. My friend Bairbre O'Flynn knows of devout north of Ireland fishermen who refuse to have their boats blessed for the same reason.

All over the British Isles the Cornish seamen's other taboo words are also shunned. No land animal is ever named on board a fishing vessel. Why, I wonder, is salmon also taboo: I have heard a trawler skipper from Kilkeel, Co. Down, refer to salmon as *cold iron man*. If ever a fisherman lets the word salmon slip out, he must say, 'Cold iron!' immediately to avert disaster. Iron is a talisman among fishermen, a symbol of strength and durability since mankind first began to use it. In some English ports *cold iron fellow* is used only of a pig.

In Cornwall, where old customs die hard, echoes of the ancient religions persist. Outsiders must think it queer that fishermen who profess a conservative Christianity would leave a little of their catch on the beach as an offering to Bucca. When the Cornish scholar Morton Nance enquired about this in both Newlyn and Mousehole he was told that the gift always disappeared overnight, and that 'as to where it was gone to, you can think what you've a mind to'. *Bucca* is not a sea god. He's the Cornish equivalent of *Puck*, the Irish word *púca* or *pooka*, the Welsh *pwca*, a mischievous being from the Otherworld.

As to how many fish it was deemed advisable to leave Bucca, nobody knew for sure, because fishermen didn't count their catch. It brought bad luck. This belief was common. In Suffolk the fishermen counted like this: 'There's a white, and a shim, and another after him, and a white, and a lily white, and a srunck-ho' (a *srunck* is a school of fish).

Three is an unlucky number among fishermen. In my young days, Co. Down fishermen would lash the second and third boats together on leaving a harbour so that they could count the fleet as numbers one, two, four, etc. I once told one of them, a devotee of the Rev. Paisley, that Cornishmen didn't like the number three either. 'Ach, them Cornishmen!' he replied. 'They are half pagan, you know, full of aul' superstitions.' He declined my invitation to have a pint with me in a cosy hostelry frequented by the lifeboat crew. Instead we went to Kilmore Quay's only restaurant where he ordered cutlets of cold iron man. His Christian faith, he said without a trace of irony, wouldn't allow him to be seen dead in a pub.

FEBRUARY 1998

MARGARET RANSON, a young lady from Norwich who is compiling a booklet of traditional recipes as one of her school projects, wrote to me for information about the origin of some culinary words. Margaret won't qualify for the title 'oldie' until about 2050 I should imagine: it was her granny, she tells me, who suggested my complicity in her work.

Walnut is the first word out of the hat. The *wal* part was originally *wealh*, which is what the Anglo-Saxons called the Welsh. So, is walnut a Welsh nut? No. *Wealh* was simply the word used by the Saxons to denote 'foreign' long before they ever came to England and bumped into the people they called Welsh and other names besides. *Wealh nut* or *walnut* simply meant the nut found in the foreign countries they were acquainted with – the lands of the Roman Empire in Italy, and Celtic Gaul. The nut they considered native to Germany was the hazel: Old English *haesel*, related to Old High German *hasala*.

One of my young friend's recipes is for *Welsh rarebit*, a dish of toasted cheese, I'm told. I have taken the liberty of suggesting that she call the dish *Welsh rabbit*, its original name. The late 18th century was the age of guesswork etymology, and it was then that 'rabbit' became 'rarebit', because rabbit made no sense. Of course it didn't; it was a joke, just as was an identical dish called *Scots rabbit*, described in a 1746 cookery book. So where's the joke? The notion was to provide a smile on meatless Fridays by pretending that these dishes were what they were not. Another example was to call a red herring *Yarmouth capon* in Margaret's neck of the woods. No such word as rarebit ever existed until it was coined by some late 18th-century chancer. Pity it survived.

Toast is an oldie. *Torrere* is the Latin for 'to dry up'; from it comes our 'torrid'. From *torrere* came the colloquial infinitive *tostare*, to scorch, to keep drying up. This *tostare*, not found in Classical Latin by the way, is the origin of our toast.

Toast was once used to flavour water and wine, and in the early 18th century it was said that a lady's name would, like toast, flavour the wine in which her health was drunk. And so the lady's name, or the lady herself, was referred to as 'a toast'. The more general sense followed by extension.

Onion is a word that has come down in the world. Its Latin antecedent was *unio*, which came from *unus*, one; *unio* was a philosopher's word denoting the abstract principle of unity. The word was subsequently purloined by the jewellers, to whom it meant a single large pearl, and according to the Spanish-Roman agriculturalist, Columella, a contemporary of Seneca, by the farmers, who used it as a slang word for the humble vegetable. Margaret uses it in her soup. In time the *u* became an *o*, but the original philosopher's sense of the word still survives in the word *union*.

Among my young friend's recipes is one for a Norfolk cocktail, a seafood mixture. *Cocktail* is of uncertain origin. It seems to have been used of drink mixtures long before it was used by chefs, and it was first recorded in print by the American, Washington Irving, in 1809. My guess is that the word derived from an older cocktail – a horse whose docked tail stood up like the tail of a cock. The fact that cocktails are supposed to be exhilarating leads me to believe that there may be a connection between the two meanings of the word.

What about margarine? The old Persian for 'pearl' was the lovely word *murwari*. The Greeks borrowed the word in the form *margarites* – whence the name Margaret, she'll be glad to know. Let us now jump forward to the 19th century when chemists began to study a substance called *margaric acid*, so called because its crystals looked like pearls, and a related substance called *margarin*, which was found to be one of the chief constituents of butter. In 1887 an Act of Parliament gave the name *margarine* to all butter substitutes. The *g*, you'll notice, should really be hard – like the *g* in Margaret, the pearl of Norwich.

MARCH 1998

HIS MEDIEVAL LATIN biography said of him: 'He was a poet, a teacher, a psalmist, a bishop, a soul friend, a noble. Nobly and honourably he went unto the angelic resting place, on the 17th of June 696, with choiring of the household of heaven, in the eighty second year of his age.'

His biographer should have mentioned that he was also a famous miller, this St Moling; and he is remembered in folklore as having succeeded in milling furze, bracken, apples and nuts into rye-flour after a disastrous harvest. He is honourably mentioned in many medieval manuscripts, including the one translated by Seamus Heaney as *Sweeney Astray*. They named one of Ireland's most beautiful places after him, a tiny hamlet on the banks of the Barrow, not far from where I grew up. They anglicized the name as St Mullins, and local people still revere him. His mill race and the remains of his mill can still be seen. He was no mythical personage. He really did exist and his Gospel Book is one of the treasures of Dublin's Trinity College library.

I spoke about him recently in a nearby village and at the conclusion of my talk I was approached by an old man who handed me a page of words. He was a mill worker once too, he said, and he wanted me to have his words before God called him to join the shades of Moling and his monks. Here are a handful of them ...

It's mildering means that it's pouring rain (the Irish never say pouring *with* rain). *Milder* is a milling term: it's the quantity of corn ground at one time. Figuratively, the milder (in some places *melder*) came to mean a great flow, a large quantity, a deluge. The phrase *dusty miller* should, according to my friend, really be *dusty milder*: it meant the last child born in a family. The *English Dialect Dictionary* (*EDD*) agrees. The Old Norse is *meldr*, flour or corn in a mill.

He called the great wooden tub into which the flour fell a *loodher*. Vigfusson's dictionary leads me to believe that the Vikings who raided St Mullins would have called it *luthr*, a flour bin.

One of my friend's expressions intrigued me. It was used by mill folk at wakes or the like, when a woman pouring out the whiskey might drown it with water. One would say: 'Easy, Mary, don't put out the miller's eye.' The *EDD* helps with this one. A correspondent from northern England wrote: 'This particular phrase has no reference to the eye of a miller, but probably to that part of the machinery of a mill termed the mill-eye. If, through the inattention of the miller, the grain flows too freely into the hopper, and thence fills the eye or aperture of the revolving stone, and brings the machinery to a stand, the mill-eye is stopped or put out.' But my man offered another explanation, also given by the *EDD*: 'The miller's eye is a hard little kernel in porridge or in bread which has not been softened by the milk or water used in its making. To put out the eye would require even more liquid, and that is why people would tell those who would drown good whiskey not to put out the miller's eye.'

The man who could lie with great fluency was said to *lie like a mill shilling*; the shilling being the shelled grain that runs out of the mill-eye. *A grain will escape the shilling* was said in reference to a black-sheep in a good family. A *mill story* was a bit of dubious gossip. A *mill clapper* was the piece of timber that struck and shook the hopper of a mill, so that 'to yap like a mill clapper' was used of a person who talked too much. The *EDD* has *mill clap*.

I promised to visit him soon and to go with him to his former workplace, now gone the way of most of the small family-owned mills: killed off by the conglomerates. 'More words will come back to me then,' he said. 'And when you've finished writing them down we'll go to Hazel's pub for a drink, and I promise not to let her put out the miller's eye in your Jameson.'

May St Moling protect me from my friends.

APRIL 1998

A YORKSHIRE FRIEND of mine startled me recently by referring to a rugby footballer who is notorious for stomping on his fallen opponents – and worse, for getting away with it – as a *Dane*. I have come across this particular racial slur in 17th- and 18th-century Irish poetry, where anybody the poet disliked was called a Danar, or Dane, be he a supporter of the Hanoverian dynasty or a man who had made a pass at his girlfriend. The fact that the gentlemen who did most of the depredation in Ireland long ago weren't Danes at all, but Norwegians, didn't seem to matter. I've often wondered what they called us, who gave as good as we got: the *Annals of Ulster* for the year 1013 tell us that an Irish king called Gilla mo-Chonna found some fair-haired blokes trespassing on his land, and having yoked most of them to a plough, forced the rest to follow, harrowing from their scrotums.

Be all that as it may, what a linguistic legacy they have left, these Norsemen. My Yorkshire friend, a retired teacher who loves his native dialect, was the ideal person to talk about words to in the corner of my local; he didn't mind in the least being bombarded with a word-list from Windhill in the West Riding, compiled by the great Joseph Wright, editor of Oxford's *English Dialect Dictionary*. Every single one of the following my friend was familiar with:

Addle, to learn. Cognate with the Old Norse *othal*, property. *Ettle*, to make a great effort. Old Norse *oetla*.

The North Country's 'a bonny bride is soon buskit' posed no problems. *Busk* is from Norse *buask*, to make oneself ready, Vigfusson's dictionary tells me. When my friend noticed that his glass was empty, he said, 'Do I have to egg you on to buy a round if it is toom?' *Toom* is from *tomr*, empty; *egg*, from Old Norse *eggja*, to entice. (Chaucer has *eggen* somewhere.)

When the drinks arrived he asked me would I like a dag in my whiskey. Old Wright had this one too, from Norfolk as well as from Yorkshire. My friend used the word figuratively: *dag* is dew; also a drizzling rain. His wife, he told me, would dag the clothes before she ironed them. The Vikings had *doegg*, dew.

Down Wright's list we went. *Trig* was faithful, reliable, he explained. The Vikings had *tryggr*. Trig is (or was) used from the North Country down as far as Hampshire and Somerset according to Wright, when speaking of recuperation from illness. 'I be trig again, thanks be God.' e e cummings's 'trig westpointer, most succinctly bred' in 'I Sing of Olaf' comes from the same source.

Yorkshiremen, I was assured, are *gleg* on the uptake. *Gloeggr* is the Viking word for clear-sighted. *Heppen*, I gathered, is one of my friend's favourite words. Joseph Wright was fond of it too. It means tidy, neat, handsome, respectable. ' "That looks heppener," is said when anything falling into disorder is satisfactorily arranged,' explained Wright. He also tells us that *heppen* is applied to linen or cotton to describe the evenness of the texture. Both Wright and my friend have *heppenly* for 'neatly'. The Norse origin was *heppinn*: lucky, also dexterous.

Apart from egg, I had never previously heard of any of the words I've mentioned. *Gain* was also new to me. 'The gainest way to Roundwood is over the hill,' said my teacher in explanation of the word that means handy, direct, least difficult. The Old Norse is *gegn*, ready, serviceable, kindly, according to Vigfusson's dictionary.

I was saddened to hear that many Yorkshire children never hear of their rich Norse legacy in their classrooms; it is, my friend said, as if the Danelaw left no marks at all. But who am I to preach? Such knowledge is not imparted in Irish schools either, and Irish English is rich in words of Viking origin. I must write to the Taoiseach.

I should, I think, also mention to him that since he has seen fit to seek the apologies of Tony Blair's government for the Great Famine of the 1840s, he should himself now apologize to the Danish crown for the antics of King Gilla mo-Chonna in 1013. The National Ploughing Championship, to be held in the Danish stronghold of Wexford in September, would be an ideal place to do the decent thing, methinks.

MAY 1998

I WILL ARISE AND GO soon, and go to Berkshire, where I have old friends who have, for twenty years at least, been tempting me to visit them. I might, while I'm there, visit Newbury to see James Cogswell who has sent me what he calls a rag-bag of Berkshire words, collected in the middle of the last century by J. Lowsley of Hampstead Norreys and published, privately, it would seem, in 1888 by his son, a major in the Royal Engineers. Mr Cogswell assures me that many of the words still survive, and I'm delighted to hear it.

Rag-bag, used figuratively nowadays in many places, was, according to Lowsley, 'a large bag hung in the kitchen of a farmhouse to receive old pieces of linen and clean cuttings from calico, etc. This rag-bag is resorted to in the case of a cut finger or in any of the numerous instances where the contents are useful.' Delicacy prevented Lowsley telling us that this was a bag used by the women of the household for storing the makings of the sanitary things they called *dollies*; woe betide the man who tampered with this hoard.

I loved too the phrase *chermin the baze* – 'An act of ringing a stone against a spade; this music is supposed to cause bees to settle in the garden; another object is to let the neighbours know who the bees belong to if they should chance to settle on adjacent property.' Chermin is from the Old English *cyrm*, a noise; *cyrman*, to make a noise.

The pronunciation of bees as baze and, I notice, of sweep as swape and treason as trayson, was, I thought in my ignorance, confined to rural Ireland. I was amused to read recently that Dr Johnson didn't know whose advice to take when he was writing his dictionary: Lord Chesterfield told him that great, for example, should be pronounced so as to rhyme with state, but Sir William Yonge insisted it should rhyme with seat, and that none but an Irishman should pronounce it grait. Chesterfield won the day, except in Ireland and, it seems, in Berkshire.

Another survival in the Berkshire countryside is *chump*, a thick piece of wood for burning. The *Oxford English Dictionary* (OED) says that this is a parallel form of *chunk*, perhaps influenced by association with *chop*, or with *lump* or *stump*. Skeat asks us to consider the Old Icelandic *kumbr*, a chopping, a cutting, and *kubba*, to cut. The word is now used figuratively to signify a dolt, a dunderhead.

A Berkshire coroner was, and still is in places, a *crowner*, a form used by Shakespeare. Both words mean simply a representative of the crown, from Latin *corona* through Anglo-French *corouner*. Richard II appointed the first crowners as keepers of the pleas of the crown; in other words, their job was to see that the crown got its financial rights. A corpse was of interest to the king's revenue men because, if a successful prosecution followed treason or murder, the miscreant's possessions went to the Exchequer. The crown also had claims on treasure-trove; this is why the king's coroners became involved with cases of this nature as well.

I wonder where the word ether (the first *e* is short) originates? *Ethers* are blackthorn rods interwoven in forming a hedge. They had a rhyme in Berkshire: 'Eldern staakye and blackthorn ether Maaykes a hedge vor years together.' *Ether* is also a dialect word for the adder; hence, I think, its connection with the spiky blackthorn hedge.

Mr Cogswell tells me that the devil is still called *Auld Gooseberry* by schoolchildren in his neck of the woods, and that the phrase 'plaayin' up auld gooseberry' is still used to indicate wild pranks, high jinks. *Louchet* also survives: it means a large piece of anything. I have no idea where it comes from. It is now a child's word, as is the charming *messenger*, 'a sunbeam coming through a long crack into a dark barn or loft'. Other children's words are *rompsin'*, rough play; *tiddle*, to feed an orphan lamb from a milk bottle; *tom*, the male of all *chickabiddies* or farmyard birds; *dall*, the smallest piglet in the litter. This is a variant of *doll*, used in Hampshire and Oxfordshire for pet piggies, and coming in a *circumbendibus* – Berkshire for a circuitous route – from Doll, pet name for Dorothy.

JUNE 1998

A SLEW (from the Irish *slua*, a crowd, from the Old Irish *slog*, an army) of letters about Welsh rabbit. One was written in that peculiar scrawl I associate with doctors' prescriptions; sure enough it was a warning from a lifelong friend who practises in London. Years of poring over medieval manuscripts have honed the skill I need to decipher my friend's letters, and soon I had deduced (a) that Welsh rabbit would have a deleterious effect on my health and (b) that Welshmen were fond of their peculiar delicacy as far back as Shakespeare's day. Have I, the lady asked, forgotten Falstaff's little exchange with Dr Evans in *Merry Wives*: 'Have I laid my brain in the sun, and dried it, that it wants matter to prevent so gross overreaching as this? Am I ridden with a Welsh goat too? ... 'Tis time I were choked with a piece of toasted cheese.'

Lay off the dairy products, this doctor ordered – a woman I have known all my life and with whom I was deeply in love until that awful summer's day she fecked an ice cream from me when we were both six. What did I do having read her advice? *Mea maxima culpa*, I went to the kitchen and tried out a recipe for Welsh rabbit sent to me from Brighton by Elizabeth Ray, the distinguished writer on wine and food. How could I resist this, which comes from Dr William Kitchiner's *The Cook's Oracle*, published in 1823:

> Cut off a slice of cheese (good fat mellow Cheshire cheese, or a double Gloster, is better than the poor single Gloster), a quarter of an inch thick, not so big as the bread by half an inch on each side. Pare off the rind. Cut out all the specks and rotten parts (rotten cheese toasted is the ne plus ultra of Hout Goût, and only eatable by the thoroughbred Gourmand, in the most inverted state of his jaded appetite), and lay it on the toasted bread in a cheese toaster. Carefully watch it, that it does not burn, and stir it with a spoon, to prevent a pellicle forming on the surface. Have ready good mustard, pepper and salt.

Delicious.

Mrs Ray takes issue with me over my guess as to the origin of *cocktail* and she has an ally in H.L. Mencken. She writes: 'Before I went there I did not know that New Orleans is the birthplace of the cocktail. At the end of the 18th century a chemist named Peychaud produced a digestive bitters that he served to customers in a double-ended egg-cup, a *coquetier*. This was much liked, especially when mixed with a tot of brandy, and soon the local agent of the Limoges brandy firm of Sazerac-de-Forge set up a coffee house in New Orleans to serve his brandy with Mr Peychaud's bitters, adding a touch of absinthe as well, and this mixture became known simply as a Sazerac. This is still very popular, although the brandy has been replaced by rye whisky, and the absinthe by Herbsaint, the local *pastis*. The *coquetier*, not difficult to mispronounce as cocktail after the second or third Sazerac, is the forerunner of the jigger used by barmen.'

Mr P.D. Hancock of Priestfield Road, Edinburgh, wrote to enquire about a word used by R.L. Stevenson in *Kidnapped* – *clappermaclaw*. The context is, 'Ye have a hang-dog, rag-and-tatter, clappermaclaw kind of look to ye.' The word is a variant of *clapperclaw*, found in Scotland and as far south as Somerset and Devon. It means, according to the *English Dialect Dictionary* – not noted for political correctness, thank God – to scratch, maul; generally used of women (especially used of beating): to abuse, scold. 'I believe 'er clapperclawed 'im shameful,' was recorded in Shropshire. Hence, *clapperclaw*, 'a noisy woman' (Devon), and *clapperclawing*, 'a round of abuse' (Shropshire).

As to *clapperclaw*'s precise meaning and origin, *Oxford* says that it means 'to claw with a clapper, though in what precise sense is not clear'. *Clapper* was a dialect word for 'hand', formed in direct imitation of the sound 'clap'; expressed in Middle English *clapper* was a rattle, related to Low German *klapper*, *klepper*. *Claw* is from Old English *clawu*, related to Middle Dutch *clauewe* and Old High German *chlawa*. As to the intrusive *ma* in Stevenson's version, it may be the Gaelic possessive pronoun *mo*, 'my' used as an intensive. I'm guessing.

JULY 1998

HOW RICH and rare is the dialect of Lancashire. I hope my tense is correct. A son of mine who worked as a GP on Merseyside for some years assures me that it is, and that all of the following words, recorded by John Nodal and George Milner in 1874 for the Manchester Literary Society, survive. My young man was in a good position to know as his practice encompassed both rural and urban areas, and rather than taking after his father, who likes to earwig in those happy hunting grounds of dialectologists, public houses, he listens in his surgery.

What do *akrans* mean to you? Well, they are acorns. The *English*

Dialect Dictionary doesn't have this form, nor the other Lancashire variant collected by Nodal and Milner, *hatchorn*. Old English had *aecern*; Gothic had the identical *akran*, meaning fruit.

The word *badger*, a keeper of a small grocery shop, is still common enough, I'm assured; it used to mean a man who sold and bought corn. In north Lancashire it meant a travelling dealer in butter and eggs. Have the supermarkets killed this one off? There was an old verb *badge*, to sell, obviously a relative, but which came first, the verb or the noun? *Oxford* dismisses Fuller's theory that it came from Latin *bajulare*, to carry.

Creawse, given in the *English Dialect Dictionary* under *crouse*, is another oldie. It means randy. It appears to be one of the figurative senses of one of the Low German or Frisian words that slipped into northern dialects early in the Middle English period, such as *drus*, which originally meant crisp. The word has reached Modern German as *krau*, crisped, curled, sullen, fractious, and into Modern Dutch as *kroes*, out of sorts, cross. Interestingly, East Frisian has *krus*, curly, entangled, and also the Lancashire sense of lascivious. Rev. Ian Paisley has been described (by a follower) as being 'as crouse as a wee banty'; in the north of Ireland *crouse* means cross, not randy, I'll have ye know.

The word *crick*, a local pain, especially one in the neck, is, I take it, as common in England as it is in Ireland. It is from the Middle English *crikke*, a spasm, but *crill*, a shiver, seems to be confined to Lancashire and Cheshire. 'Look down on these poor people, it's enough to make you crill,' is a line from a Lancashire ballad of Cobbett's time. Nodal and Milner don't hazard a guess as to the word's origin, which is no great harm, to judge from many of their efforts in this line. The great *OED* doesn't have the word, which is surprising, but for what it's worth I think it's Norse in origin. There is the Danish *kriller*, which means, approximately, to have the creeps.

I wonder how many words there are in English for a slovenly woman? The Irish *streel* is the Lancashire *dossy* and her sister, *dossuck*. Are dossucks given to *gawstering*, boasting and swaggering? This is the same word as Middle English *galstren*, to make a noise.

Hanch-apple is a nice homely word. We call it snap-apple. On the other side of the border the Scots called Hallowe'en *hanching night*. The word is from the French *hancher*, to snap with the teeth, according to Randle Cotgrave.

Greet is still to be heard in parts of Liverpool, I'm assured; it means to weep. 'Give o'er the greetin' or I'll give you cause to greet,' a sensible granny was heard saying to her young grandson who, after attempting to demolish a doctor's waiting-room, got a warm backside for his pains and resorted to wailing. Greet can be traced back to Old English *graetan*, to weep. Old Norse had *grata*.

A kiss is a *cuss* in many places in Lancashire. *Cuss* is also the mouth. *Cuss-cat* is a nickname. Often written *kuss*, the word comes directly from Old English *coss*. Too much kussing no doubt causes creaws boys to make bash Lancashire girls greet. *Bash*, abash, embarrassed, confused, can be traced back through Old French to Vulgar Latin *batare*, to gape at, examine closely. And that's enough sex for one day.

AUGUST 1998

BARRY FLOYD from Wymondham in Norfolk has sent me some interesting words culled from the Rev. Robert Forby's *The Vocabulary of East Anglia*, published in 1830. I was delighted to hear a young Norfolk friend say that she recognized many of them.

One such is *arsle*, to fidget, especially on a seat. There was quite a bit of arsling going on in Rev. Forby's church, I'd say, as his sermons tended to last an hour at least. Strangely enough, the word is not in Joseph Wright's great *English Dialect Dictionary*.

The *clim* is a sort of imp that inhabits the chimneys of nurseries and is sometimes called down to take away naughty children. Wright's *EDD*, published in 1898, says that the word was then obsolete; not so, says my young Norfolk friend, Jane Nash, who was more than once threatened with a visit from the clim when she was a mauther.

A *mauther* is a girl, Forby explains; an adolescent girl, Jane insists. The *EDD* gives this gloss: 'A girl just growing into womanhood, especially a great, rough, awkward wench; an unmarried woman; also used of mares, cows and other female animals.' Ben Jonson in *The Alchemist* has, 'Away, you talk like a foolish mauther.' Is there a Norse connection here? Norwegian dialect has the phrase *moder, mor!* used in calling girls, and the *EDD* gives *moder* as a variant of *mawther*.

A Norfolk *flazzard* is 'a stout, broad-faced woman dressed in a loose flaring manner', according to Rev. Forby. I wonder if this word is related to John Clare's *flaze*, a smoky flame: 'Forcing bright sparks to twinkle from the flaze.'

Mortal is a word that is used as an intensive far from Rev. Forby's Norfolk: it means great, serious. I've heard 'He's a mortal prat,' in reference to Master P. Gascoigne. Hence, *mortal rags* are tatters, shreds, in Cornwall. The word also means dead drunk; a Gallowayman reported to the *EDD* that a friend was 'often carried home mortal on a hand-barrow'; and a correspondent from Northumberland told Wright: 'The pilgrim was drunk when he went oot, and he came back mortal.'

A *ringle* was a little ring in Norfolk, and in Suffolk too; to be *ringled* is to be married. The lovely word still lives, I'm glad to hear. Wright has it.

What an extraordinary man the *EDD*'s Joseph Wright was. He was born in 1855 and, because his father died young, his childhood was spent slaving in a Bradford mill to support the family. He taught himself, in the evenings, to read and write in English, French and German. In 1876 Wright set out for Heidelberg with £40 in his pocket, returning there for a six-year stint in 1882. There he mastered the new science of comparative philology. In 1888 Oxford gave him a small lecturing job; and a full chair in 1901. I am pleased to say that my own *alma mater*, Trinity College Dublin, gave him his first honorary doctorate in 1906.

In 1873 the English Dialect Society began collecting words with a dialect dictionary as the ultimate object. This was to be a supplement to the *Oxford English Dictionary*, which was to deal mainly with standard words. By the time the society was wound up in 1896 it had been the means of publishing eighty regional glossaries.

Wright was the obvious choice to edit the new dialect dictionary. He was presented with a million card indexes, weighing one ton, by the English Dialect Society. To help him sift through these, the sacks of newspaper cuttings, the private collections of words, the countless words of poetry and fiction that might contain dialect words, and the glossaries old and new, he collected an army of 600 amateur helpers.

He had to set up a campaign to lure private subscribers. These were asked to pay a pound a year and would receive in return two

'Getting Ringled to a Hazzard.'

sections of the new work per annum. Balfour gave him a Civil List pension, and the Royal Bounty provided £600 to speed the publication of the six volumes of his monumental work. It took him ten years.

He was working on a paper on the English of Norfolk when he passed away in the summer of 1930. May God look to him.

SEPTEMBER 1998

NOT ALL of my readers will have heard of Father Patrick Dinneen, S.J. He appears briefly in Joyce's *Ulysses* as the author of a famous Irish-English dictionary, a work that has given me much pleasure over the years. Flann O'Brien, author of the comic masterpiece *At Swim-Two-Birds*, described Dinneen's work as a comic dictionary, but for all its idiosyncrasies it is a brilliant, encyclopaedic piece of scholarship, which often rambles down the *loanings* (Ulster and Scottish lanes) of world mythology and folklore.

One of the reasons why Flann O'Brien thought the book comical was that its author didn't bother to separate each word's various meanings, as *Oxford* and all the great modern dictionaries do. Dinneen was merely following most of the earlier lexicographers, O'Reilly, for example, who gave us *luan*: a loin, a kidney, a son, a lad, a hero, a champion, a woman's breast, a greyhound, a dog, the moon, and *clith*: left-handed, close, true, just, a desire for copulation in cattle. The following, from Dinneen, tickled O'Brien's fancy – *geineog*: a female infant, a sprout, a foreign growth, a midwife, a gem, and *sagairtín*: a little priest, a small inedible periwinkle.

No doubt this would give Mr Sammy Wilson, the Belfast intellectual who called Irish a leprechaun language, reason to think that he was right, but please consider the following:

> a fixed look; a square stone; a badger's burrow; a number of couples at a dance; a church service; a determined attempt to

get a man's affections; a sucker; a political party; a portion of a potato; a pair of bagpipes; a religious body; a game of dice; a complement of teeth; a team of horses, etc.

The headword? Set. The source? *Oxford*. The layout is as it would have been had not Murray determined that the various meanings in his great dictionary be given as 1,2,3, etc.

It is rather more difficult to forgive Dinneen for using the present tense instead of the infinitive, which gave us the following beauties: 'I flow, I rush in streams'; 'I give birth to a still-born calf'; 'I copulate, as swine.'

In Dinneen we have a feminist's *bête noir*, the most politically incorrect lexicographer of them all. One headword was defined as 'a fat cow, a lazy woman'; another as 'a piggish woman', explained by the further gloss, 'a woman is like a pig in her obstinacy'. To the verb that means to conceive he adds an Irish phrase, which he translates as 'not to blessedness was woman born'.

As I said, he loved to throw in bits of folklore, even when the folklore has nothing much to do with the word being explained. The word for a lump of meat was explained adequately, and then he tells us that 'the difference in the length of Christmas and Little Christmas (12 January) is the time taken to singe a goose with lighted straw'. And when dealing with *meann*, the Irish for stuttering, he said that the word was also the origin of the surname Minn, and that a large percentage of stutterers existed amongst people of this name in Liverpool. Kuno Meyer, the great Celticist, told him that.

What a book! It's almost worth learning Irish to read it.

It was a letter from Mr James Dinneen of Santry, Dublin, that brought his illustrious namesake to mind. James wants to know the origin of *swale*, a word he never heard until it was used by American commentators at the British Open Golf Championship to describe a depression near the green. It travelled from Scotland to America; often spelled *swaill*, it originally meant a shady place, and it has a Norse origin. Compare Old Icelandic *svalr*, cool.

From J.S. Reville in Oldham comes a query about the verb *to lig*, to lie down. An oldie this; it too is of Norse origin. Chaucer has, 'The plowman plucked up his plowe When Midsomer morn was comen in, And saied his bestes should ete inowe, And lige in grass up to the chin.' The Old Icelandic was *ligg*, from the Gothic *liggan*. I'm tempted to say that had Father Dinneen glossed it, he would have added something like, 'The silly cow of a woman ligged in the swail with the young god.' And then he would have given us instances from Indian, Greek, Celtic and Nordic mythology about silly cows who did just that, and enjoyed it.

OCTOBER 1998

CAPTAIN WILLIAM J. GORTA of the New York Police Department has spent the last year in England, teaching this and that to various police authorities. He is Columbia-educated and is quite an authority on the English of his native city. He recently gave me a copy of a fascinating book by Herbert Asbury called *The Gangs of New York*; written in 1928 it deals with what the English, Irish, Italians and Jews got up to between the Revolution and the sad demise of Owen 'The Killer' Madden in the 1920s. An appendix to this book gives some of the entries in *Vocabulum* or *The Rogue's Lexicon*, collected and published by George Matsell, Chief of the New York City Police in 1859.

Matsell collected his words in the Bowery, Five Points and Paradise Alley sections of the city, where at various times during the first half of the 19th century the Kerryonians, the Plug Uglies, the O'Connell Guards and the True Blue Americans ruled the streets. I am sorry to have to tell you that most of the gentlemen who ran the gangs I've just mentioned were natives of the Emerald Isle. Neither Captain Gorta nor I can explain how their gangland lingo, although it has, occasionally, a distinctly Irish flavour as we shall see, reeks (if that's the word I'm looking for) of London's much more salubrious Seven Dials.

The early gangs were bred in a dreadful poverty that shocked even Dickens: 'Where dogs would howl to lie, men and women slink off to sleep, forcing the dislodged rats to move away to better lodgings ... all that is loathsome, drooping and decaying is here.'

In the course of time, the gangland argot was supplemented by words and phrases from Yiddish and Italian. I give here only words that came from England and Ireland. Some of them have survived.

Ace of Spades: a widow. Partridge says that this term was never current in England. It is still used in New York. *Baptized*: liquor that has been watered down. Partridge could find no trace of this usage in England before 1921. Small wonder – it is a calque from Irish Gaelic slang *baistithe*. *Bat*: a night-walking prostitute. Recorded in England in 1811; gone now from New York speech. *Bleak*: handsome. The word is still common in New York and now unknown on this side of the pond. It was formed by antiphrasis, or deliberate perversion of *bleached mort*, a very fair girl, and it was first seen in print in England in *A New Canting Dictionary* in 1725. *Blowen*: the mistress of a thief. The word is still common in Terry Wogan's Limerick; the great man is the darling of many's the sooty blowen in his native city. *Sooty blowen* means dark beauty; and blowen comes from the German *blühen*, to bloom or blossom. The New York and English cant meaning, a thief's mistress or a whore, is a debasement of a lovely word.

Booley dog was a Paradise Alley word for a policeman. This is surely Irish in origin. Booley is from Irish *buaile*, an enclosure where cattle were kept for milking. In the Bowery, a booley was a prison. The New York *cat*, a whore, was in English cant in the 16th century; so was the verb *to mow*, to have sex with a woman. *Lady bird* and *left-handed wife* were terms for mistress. English cant doesn't have them.

Music was a verdict of not guilty; the term didn't travel from New York. You'll still hear *gander*, a married man not living with his wife, in Dublin slang; and the Paradise Alley *ground sweat*, a grave, is found in the great Dublin underworld song of the 1780s, 'The Night Afore Larry Was Stretched'.

Asbury gives the words of a lovely street song that was made up in the Alley in its worst days. Even there love blossomed:

> *She's had offers to wed by the dozen, 'tis said,*
> *Still she's always refused them politely;*
> *But of late she's been seen with young Tommy Killeen,*
> *Going out for a promenade nightly.*
> *We can guess all the rest, for the boy she loves best,*
> *Will soon change her name from MacNally;*
> *Though he may change her name, she'll be known just the same,*
> *As the Sunshine of Paradise Alley.*

Master Wogan might like to know that she too was born in Limerick.

NOVEMBER 1998

I WENT DOWN to my own part of Ireland recently. I was anxious to have a chat with an old cooper, the last of the craftsmen who made the wooden plates, cups, saucers and bowls formerly used in the Anglo-Norman baronies of south-east Wexford. 'You are too late,' a friend of his informed me, with a hint of reproach in his voice. 'He's ago.'

I am reliably informed that this past participle is still used in Devon when country people mean gone or finished. A love affair might be ago, or the blooms might be ago from her cheeks; but Chaucer used it in *The Legend of Good Women* as my friend had used it: 'And thus are Tisbe and Piramus ago.' Dead, in other words.

I'd like to thank the many people who have written to me about words. Mrs Joan Prince from Bodmin, Cornwall, tells me that in her mother's day to be *charming* meant to be in good health. This usage is found too in Gloucestershire and Somerset; and the *EDD* recorded, 'I be quite chermin, thank ee,' in Devon.

Another of Mrs Prince's words that took my fancy was *chet*, a kitten. She also sent a little bit of folklore about these chets: 'My mother would never allow us to keep chets born in the month of May on the farm. People of her generation believed that they would infest the outhouses with worms and that they would entice rats and mice into the dwelling-house. So, May chets were drowned at birth.'

I notice that the word also took the form *chat* in Cornwall and neighbouring counties and that there was also a verb *to chat*, which meant to have kittens. Hence *chetten*, to bring forth young, used of cats, hares and rabbits. Mrs Prince tells me that in parts of Devon chat is an affectionate term for a child. Another oldie, this. Grose has it in his 1790 dictionary. I suppose the pronunciation here is influenced somewhat by French *chat* and *chaton*, kitten.

Palsh is another of Mrs Prince's words. This too was new to me, but the dialect dictionaries have it. An adjective, it originated in Cornwall, but is also found in Devon. To my correspondent it means in poor health, always ailing, frail. She doesn't mention the word as a verb, but it has been recorded as such, with the meaning to mend, to patch up clothes; figuratively, to half-cure a sick person. The *EDD* has 'A poor palched creature,' from Cornwall. The word is from Old Cornish, *palch* – weak, sickly, making a poor recovery, according to Williams's dictionary.

I'll finish with a word that has survived in many dialects since 1450 at least, when we find it in *The Wars of Alexander*, 'Backis ... biggir and hardere than any comon cogill-stane.' A *coggle* is a round, smooth stone, a cobblestone. The word's origin is unknown, I'm sorry to have to tell Dr Ruth Blake of Leicester. This good lady reminds me that coggle has another meaning in Dublin, where she read medicine at our College of Surgeons. She relates the following story, in impeccable Dublinese, about Dean Swift. I myself have heard versions of it.

The Dane [Dublin pronunciation] brought home a quare fella one night to give him supper. He was a musicianer or something. The Dane had a servant be the name of Jack, and he didn't like it one bit when his reverence sat his guest down to share a supper of two lovely plump partridges with him. The Dane left the room for a minute, and Jack decided to polish off one of the birds himself. That didn't satisfy him. He then ate the second one, and says to the guest: 'You are some fool to come here with the mad Dane. He's gone out now to sharpen the carving knife to cut the two coggles off you.' With that the Dane comes back, sharpening the carving knife and looking very happy, and Jack pipes up, 'Your man ate the two partridges on you, sir,' he says. Off goes the guest as if the divil was after him, and the Dane shouting, 'Come back here, sir! Give me one of them! All I want is *one* of them!' 'Go to blazes, you mad bastard!' shouted the musicianer back at him. 'I want the two of them meself!'

Has Victoria Glendinning heard that one?

DECEMBER 1998

I TRAVELLED TO London last month to see my granddaughter, Mary, christened. I'll probably spend Christmas Day there, having spent Chewidden Day in Cornwall with another son.

Chewidden Day is the Thursday of the week preceeding Christmas Day and it commemorates the occasion when black tin was first smelted, by fusion, into white. Saint Chewidden used to be held in veneration by the miners as the person to whom Saint Piran or Perran gave the news of the discovery of tin. *Chiwidden* in Old Cornish means white house – that is, a smelting house. *Chi* stood for *ti, ty*, house; *gwidn* meant white, earlier *gwyn*. I have another *cheeld-vean* in Newquay. This is a term of endearment; Old Cornish *vean, vyan*, meant little, a mutation of *byhan, byan, bechan*. The Welsh is *bychan*. *Cheeld*, of course, is a Cornish child.

Many old and dear friends of mine are intent on cosseting me during Christmas and the New Year. A Yorkshire couple wrote to ask me to share their *Yule Mart* with them. This is an ox killed and salted for Christmas and the remaining winter months. *Mart* is Irish and Scots Gaelic for beef; the dialect dictionaries, even Wright's great one, don't even hazard a guess as to where the Old Irish word came from. Surely this is the same word as *mart*, meaning a dead body; hence in a restricted sense, an ox or cow slaughtered for meat. It is derived from Latin *mortuus*, as you may have guessed.

This Yule Mart was new to me; so too are many of the culinary terms we are given in *The Scots Thesaurus* published by Aberdeen University Press, a splendid work edited by Iseabail Macleod, Pauline Cairns, Ruth Martin and Caroline Macafee, who has already given us *The Ulster Dialect Dictionary*.

The *Pope's Eye* is a cut of beef from the animal's hip, corresponding to the English rump. *Sey* or *say* is a cut of beef from the shoulder to the loin, corresponding to the English steak or sirloin. *Kirnels* are cooked animal glands – lambs' testicles, for example. If you like scrambled eggs, just ask for *caddle* in Perth; or you might like to try *drappit egg* – one poached in gravy made from the liver of a fowl. That sounds interesting, and sorry about the cholesterol, Doctor.

Hogmanay in Scotland can be hard on the liver, but I am informed that *wangrace* is a good cure, and far better than the traditional hair of the dog. This is thin gruel sweetened with fresh butter and honey. My wife, God look to her, had this word from her native Donegal. It is taken at bedtime as a remedy against the common cold, and in the old days was given to women after childbirth.

Oatmeal was a common ingredient in so many Christmas delicacies in days gone by. I was surprised to find *parkin* in the Aberdeen thesaurus: 'A hard, round, ginger-flavoured biscuit made of oatmeal, flour and treacle with an almond in the centre.' This is a delicacy usually associated with Yorkshire, Henderson's *Folk Lore* (1879) tells me: 'On the 5th of November parkin, a sort of pepper-cake, made with treacle and ginger, is found in every house in the West Riding.' My Wexford grandmother made them with honey instead of treacle, and on Christmas Eve. She called them *honey perkins*.

Which brings me back to the christening I mentioned. Iseabail Macleod and her colleagues have the delightful *dreaming bread*. I knew of the custom of putting a little bit of the christening cake under the child's pillow to ensure the sweetest of dreams forever; isn't dreaming bread lovely?

Another custom, forgotten now I suppose, was the North Country one of taking a slice of the christening cake along to the church and offering it to the first person met on the journey. Should this be a man, the next child born in the village would be male, they believed; if a woman, it would be a female. In Scotland the offering was called a *christening bit*.

But it's the Christmas bits I look forward to now, and the pudding – which we in Wexford called *Cutlin Porridge* – and whatever else they think up for me in London and Cornwall. Have a nice Christmas, and as they say in Co. Carlow, *fan óg*, pronounced 'fonogue' – stay young: young at heart and content.

JANUARY 1999

JANUARY IS KNOWN in Ireland and in Scotland as the *Black Month*. It is, or was, known in Scotland and in England's North Country as *Janiveer*, in Shropshire as *Janiwerry*, in Surrey as *Jiniver* and in Norfolk as *Janwar*. We know these dialect words from folklore. 'The blackest month in all the year is the month of Janiveer'; 'A Janiveer spring is worth naething'; 'If the grass grows in Janiveer, 'Twill be the worse for't a' the year'; 'March in Janiveer, Janiveer in March I fear'; 'Jack Frost in Janiveer nips the nose of the nascent year'; 'Janwar's day creeps in, just like a peevish auld gray man'; 'Janiwerry-freeze-the-pot-by-the-fire'; 'If the calends of Jiniver be smiling and gay, you'll have wintry weather till the calends of May'; 'Jiniver poults never come to no good'; 'Who in Jiniver sows oats, gets gold and groats.'

Yes, the folklore is extensive. If you live in Sussex, you might consider going out at midnight on the eve of the feast of St Hilary (14 January), traditionally believed to be the coldest night of the year, and bringing in a matchbox-full of mud from the garden. This you should keep in a safe place near the fire; it ensures health and happiness for a year and a day. They had a name for it in Sussex long ago – *January butter*. But can anybody tell me why the Essex farmers used to call their working horses January?

Reference I made last month to the lovely *dreaming bread*, a bit of christening cake put under a baby's pillow to ensure sweet dreams, and to the *christening bit*, a slice of christening cake given away on the journey to the church, brought some interesting letters. I am delighted to tell you that these customs survive still in parts of Scotland. In Cornwall the christening bit had more of a pagan function, and I am grateful to Mrs Jane Hall of Truro for a quotation from a glossary of Cornish words collected for the English Dialect Society in 1880 by Courtney and Couch:

> *Kimbly*: A gift, commonly a piece of bread, offered at christenings and weddings. The term refers to a curious custom which probably at some time was general, but now exists only at Polperro. When the parties set out from the house to go to the church one person is sent before them with this selected piece of bread in his or her hand, and the piece is given to the first individual that is met, whose attention has been drawn to the principal parties. I interpret it to have some reference to the evil eye, and its influence from envy which might fall upon the child, and which is sought to be averted by this unexpected gift.

I don't know the origin of the word kimbly, which also had the meaning a handsel for good news, such as the news of a birth, or good news related to smuggling or, the Lord save us, to a shipwreck.

Caroline Bradshaw from Liverpool sent me the term christening saup to complement the christening bit. *Saup*, the Wexford *zap* and the Yorkshire *sope* are all variants of *sup*. The Old English is *sopa*; the Old Norse *sopi*, a mouthful, a sup. Caroline's *christening saup* was the dram given at what the Scots call the *kimmering*, the christening party, to the proud mother, who drank it in three sups, in the name of the Father, the Son and the Holy Ghost. This party was also known in Scotland as *cummer-skolls*. It was for relatives and friends, while the party given privately by the family for the woman who has just had the baby was called *cummer-fealls*. *Skolls* are toasts, as any Norwegian will tell you. *Fealls*, I think, may be related to Old French, *feal*, loyal. *Cummer* and *kimmer* mean a godmother. From Old French *commere*, glossed by an ancient source as the woman who brings the baby to the church.

Ruth James from Douglas in the Isle of Man wrote to ask where her mother's words, *soorey*, courtship, and *soorying*, courting, originated. The accent is on the first syllable. These are Gaelic words. Compare the Irish *suirí*, courtship, pronounced (more or less) *siree*, with the accent on the first syllable.

A happy New Year to you all.

FEBRUARY 1999

ISN'T IT STRANGE, to say the least, that the farmers of yesteryear cursed a fair February? The harsher the weather was in this month, the more they rejoiced, so their proverbs tell us. 'All the moneths in the year curse a fair Februeer,' the Englishman Ray's *Proverbs*, published in 1678, assures us. He goes on to tell us that 'the Welchman had rather see his dam on the beer than to see a fair Februeer'. In Scotland 12–14 February were called the *Borrowed Days*, borrowed from January, you see; and for some reason it was thought to be a good omen if floods, snow, ice, thunderbolts, lightning, and everything else the heavens are capable of sending us visited at this time.

Well, while the farmers were praying for disasters, their good wives were hard at work in the kitchen making Florentines and such treats to keep the cold at bay. Florentines were a favourite treat in the old days and they were particularly associated with February, Mary Joly tells me; she wrote from Hampstead where she lives in exile, far from her native Aberdeen.

In Scotland, a *Florentine* was a veal or grouse pie, but in Bedfordshire they had a dish called *Apple Florentine*, a favourite both at Christmas and at ploughmen's suppers in this vicious month. This confection, a Year Book of 1841 informs us, consisted of an immensely large dish of pewter filled to the brim with good baking apples, sugar and lemon, with a roll of rich paste as a covering, pie-fashion. When baked, the upper crust was removed and used to garnish the dish; then a full quart of hissing-hot spiced ale was poured on the mess. Delicious, by all accounts. I must tell them at Simpson's-in-the-Strand, *The Oldie*'s favourite restaurant, where they still use pudding instead of dessert. The origin of *pudding*, by the way, is uncertain. Compare the French *boudin*, stuffed sausage, Old English *puduc*, a wart, and *puddewurst*, black pudding. As for *dessert*, this word is from Middle French *dessert*, removal of the main course, from *desservir*, clear the table, from *des-*, 'un-' in English, plus Old French *servir*, to serve.

Ray Fenn wrote to me from Shotesham, Norwich, about some interesting Norfolk words. I had mentioned that *chat* was a Cornish kitten, but in Norfolk, Mr Fenn tells me, a *chat* was a flea, and to say of somebody that he was *suffen* (rather) *chatty* would have meant that he was verminous rather than having a predilection for gossip.

But *chates* in the language of Norfolk means 'little pieces (there appears to be no singular form), usually with reference to trimmings or parings from some larger entity: for example, the pieces trimmed from turnips, say, to prepare them for animal feed', according to Mr Fenn. What an interesting old word this is. *Piers Plowman* has it as both *chetes* and *escheytes*, property falling to the king. The Anglo-French was *eschaetes*, forfeitures, derived from *chaet*, past participle of *chaoir* (Modern French *choir*).

A friend of mine who lives near Norwich occasionally regales me with anecdotes related in broad Norfolkese, which have to be translated for me. She would be amused by the following exchange reported by Mr Fenn as having occurred in the shadow of the great cathedral on a miserable winter's day. A Norwich matron observed a gentleman erecting an automatic umbrella, a piece of equipment she had never seen before:

> *She (astonished)*: 'Dew thet dew thet?'
> *He*: 'Thet dew.'

An irksome time of the year this for oldies, with many of us troubled by hoozes and hoasts. If you live in the North Country you'll probably know that a *hooze* is a dry cough that sometimes leads to difficulty in breathing, and that a *hoast* is also a cough, a hoarseness, a cold on the chest or in the throat. G.F. Smyth sent me those two words from Ayr, and I've since seen them in Yorkshire and Lancashire glossaries. Hooze is from Old English *hwosan*, to wheeze. Hoast is also found as *host*, *hoost* and *houst* in Ireland; it's from Old English *hwosta* and Old Norse *hósta*, a cough.

A jorum of punch is your only man for hoozes and hoasts; *jorum*, I'm sure you know, is from the proper name Joram, in allusion to that chap's connection with 'vessels of silver, and vessels of gold, and vessels of brass' in the Bible – in *Solomon*, I think. Anyway, cheers!

MARCH 1999

MY FAVOURITE OLDIE died just before Christmas. His name was Jack Devereux and he was nearly ninety. He was a retired fisherman, a lifeboatman when those crafts were open boats powered by oarsmen, an antiquarian and an important folklorist though he had left school at thirteen. His contribution to the culture of his native place was recognized in 1991 when the National University of Ireland conferred an honorary MA on him.

He came from Kilmore Quay, in the Barony of Bargy in south-east Wexford, in south-east Ireland, facing the Atlantic. Here the Anglo-Normans landed and here they stayed, rarely mixing with the Irish until Cromwell came to cut a bloody swathe through them, sending the old families west of the Shannon River to the poor province of Connacht. The Act of Settlement promised them their lands back, but Charles II decided otherwise; yet the Devereux family returned and settled down as tenant farmers on the estates of the usurpers, retaining their own customs and speaking, until the middle of the last century, their own brand of archaic English that they called Yola, their word for 'old'. Jack Devereux's family could trace its roots back to the Dukes of Normandy and the Conqueror, and he once told me that this knowledge encouraged him to read widely and to help preserve what he remembered of the ancient dialect spoken by his ancestors. The following is a sampling of his words. Some of them are of obscure origin; they must have come from somewhere in Britain, probably from the south-west, and perhaps readers can help me identify their places of origin.

Amain: 'Goin' on amain', getting on well. Compare Old English *maegn*. He remembered the old plural *-en* in *ashen*, ashes. Chaucer has, 'Other colour than asshen hath she noon.' *Bail*: this, he said, was 'a fastening for cattle in a stall; the upright sticks for that purpose'. The word is from Old French *baille*, from Latin *baculum*.

Balcoot: a waterhen. Can anybody help identify the origin of the first element? *Bibbern*: shivering. The Middle Dutch was *bibberen*. *Boldoon*: a tomcat. Origin unknown to me. *The bow*: the banshee. This is from Irish. Jack also used the word when speaking of a bad female singer, a bar-room coloratura. *Grassnaythe*: 'The stay for a scythe blade, between blade and handle.' Origin unknown to me.

His word for a hollow was *hel*, from Middle English *hol*, I suppose. *Helt*: this meant covered. 'The potatoes are helt to protect them from the frost.' From Old English *helan*, Middle English *helen*.

But where did the following come from? *Minnymay*, sugar; *scrimsher*, a miser; *sherogany*, a crowd; *shrump*, a hollow in a field; *turmit*, a turnip; *sangals*, 'the leavings in a cornfield, gathered by hand, before the days of the combined harvester'; *pulmare*, 'an untilled pathway between plots in a field; between the wheat and barley crops for instance'; *rayship*, satisfactory information ('I could get no rayship out of her'); and *raacoons*, 'small rain clouds travelling fast before a storm'.

The north-flowing tide he called the *norstrum*; the south-flowing tide, the *soustrum*. Compare the Dutch *stroom*, the German *strom*. *To baaze* meant 'to walk against the storm; to beat against the storm in a boat'. Again, I don't know where this word came from.

Not long before he died he solved a problem that had troubled me for years. A version of the Lord's Prayer in Yola, written down in 1876 by a local schoolteacher, contained the 'Protestant' addendum. The manuscript, however, had been tampered with by a mad scholar who happened to be a Protestant, and the prayer was in his hand. A fake, an exercise in composition, I thought. Not so, said Jack. He identified the prayer as the version said by a friend of his great-grandfather's, a Protestant labourer. He asked me to recite it at his funeral Mass. I did so. This is it: *Oure vaader fho yarth ing heaveene, ee-halloweth be t'naume. Thee kingdome coome, thee weel be ee-doane, as ing heaveene, zo eake an earthe. Yee ouze todeie oure deilye breed, an varyee ouze oure dettores; an lead ouze nat ing to varsaaken, mot varlouse ouze vram evil. Vur theen an ee kingdome an ee creft and ee lordlyeheed, ing ayeheede. Amein.*

APRIL 1999

ONCE UPON A TIME, and a long time ago it was, I had a few drinks with supporters of an English rugby team that had trounced our lot in nearby Lansdowne Road. Singing is not unusual on such occasions but I raised an eyebrow when my new-found friends broke into a dance, which was accompanied by words immediately recognizable as those of a mumming play. It turned out that these revellers were from Coventry, a city that has preserved a great medieval mumming tradition to this day. Years afterwards I saw the real Coventry Mummers in action. A friend of mine was instrumental in bringing them to a Co. Wexford village to perform and they brought the house down.

Jack Gosling wrote to me from Coventry recently and his letter brought back memories of that memorable night in Broadway village. He asked about the word *kex-flute,* a home-made instrument used by children in his father's time.

Kex is not known in Ireland, and I'm told that it is rare in Scotland. There is a reference to *kex-whistle* in the *English Dialect Dictionary*. An entry from Warwickshire states: 'Kex-whistles are distinguished by this name from whistles made of small branches of the willow from which the wood could be easily removed.'

Kex, or *kecks*, are hollow-stalked umbelliferous plants, and particularly the dried stalks of such plants; umbelliferous plants, in case you are as ignorant of the science of botany as I am, are a family of plants typically having hollow stems, divided or compound leaves and flowers in *umbels* or clusters, a word derived from *umbella*, the Latin for sunshade.

John Clare knew that the fairies lived in such plants: 'They venture from their dwellings once again, From keck-stalk cavity or hollow bean.' Country people made good use of them. Boys made miniature windmills from the dried split stalks of the nettle. In *Notes and Queries* of 1878 a correspondent wrote nostalgically:

> A favourite amusement with us was kex-shooting. We made bows, and then betook ourselves to a nettle bed where the kexes stood, and cutting them close by to the ground trimmed them and shot them away from the bow against the wind at an angle which carried them so high that often they went out of sight.

Bees were fed with kecks filled with sugar introduced into their hives. Hollow elder-kecks were used as moulds for home-made candles in Cobbett's time. Bean-stalk kecks were used for catching earwigs in peach, pear, plum and cherry trees trained to grow up walls.

An old word this, of uncertain origin. *Piers Plowman* has, 'As doth a kex or candel ... hath fyre and blaseth.' Some of the major dictionaries say that it may be from Welsh *cecys* (plural); nonsense, this: the Welsh word is from the English. Beaumont and Fletcher used it in the figurative sense of a sapless, innervated person in *King & No King*: 'I'll make these withered kexes bear my body two hours together above ground.'

In a butcher's shop in Gloucester Joyce Erskine recently heard an oldie issue a stern warning to the man on the other side of the counter. 'I want meat, not keech, this time, do you hear?' *Keech* is fat. I'm glad it has survived, if only because Shakespeare used it in *Henry VIII*: 'I wonder that such a keech can with his very bulk, Take up the rays o' the beneficial sun, And keep it from the earth.' He has *tallow catch* in *Henry IV, Part I*. A variant, I suppose. Origin uncertain.

For an oldie to be called *olived* in northern Ireland is to be paid a compliment. The word means lively, full of beans, the life and soul of the party. It is derived from literary English *alive* and I mention it for no better reason than that it came into my head as I read a letter from Joan Warren of Lincoln who asks about the old saying, 'That beats Oliver and Oliver beat Long Crown!'

The *EDD* cites Thompson's *History of Boston* (1856) to throw light on Joan's saying: 'It beats old Oliver (Cromwell), and he beat the Cavaliers, called high or long crowns, from the shape of their hats.'

I am attempting to compile a glossary of words of Old Norse origin still used in the dialects of these islands. I need all the help I can get, so come all ye olived oldies who live wherever the Vikings once held sway.

MAY 1999

I WAS TRAWLING the other day through a variety of dialect dictionaries trying to help a lady who wrote to me from Yorkshire about the word mister, when I came on the word Miss, now, alas, quickly being made redundant. I was amused to find that *Miss* was the title given to a married woman in parts of rural Sussex until quite recently, single women being addressed as Mrs. *Miss* also meant a mistress, a paramour. This naughty Miss seemed to be confined to Scotland; a church history of 1817, castigating the nobles of the south for their randy ways, said that, 'It was thought nothing uncivil for the peers of England to talk of their popish Misses in their houses of Parliament, even before the King's face.'

Kate Scott's *mister* is not a male Miss, Mrs or even Ms; it is most often heard in the phrase *what mister?*, which means what kind? what sort? An old phrase this, as old as Chaucer, who has, 'But telleth me what mister men yue been' in *The Canterbury Tales*. The phrase *what mister men?* is equivalent to *men of what mister?* and mister is from Old French *mestier*, 'genre d'occupation manuelle', according to my dictionary.

I had never come across Mrs Scott's word; but I was familiar with a Scots *mister*, which meant need, want, necessity. The *English Dialect Dictionary* says that this word is obsolete; however, I have been informed that it is no such thing, and that in the unlikely event of my ever being asked to go deer-stalking with him in Balmoral, I may hear Your Man's gillies use the word frequently.

Another Scott has this in *Midlothian*, 'Warld's gear was henceforth the least of her care, nor was it likely to be muckle her mister.' His contemporary, Hogg, had *mister* as a verb meaning to need, to be necessary. In his 1838 *Tales* he wrote, 'Little misters to me what they gang.' The noun, as old in English as the *Cursor Mundi* of c. 1300, which has, 'With tresour greet & preciouse thing Suche as maydenes han of mistere,' comes from Norman French *mestier*, want, necessity.

43

I have long ago ceased to be amazed to hear words considered obsolete by the dictionaries. Sometime last year in a Dublin hospital a woman spoke to me about the kindness of a young nurse who had dressed her wounds, or *pansed* them, as she put it. This too is ancient, and originally French. Randle Cotgrave's great French-English dictionary of 1611 gives the word's origin as *panser*, to dress, attend to.

I wonder is the Cornish *wink*, a well from which water is drawn by a winched bucket, obsolete by now? Judy Ross, a Cornish-woman who now lives in Croydon, wants to know something about the word's origin. *Wink* (*wenk* in Somerset) is also the word for the winch used at the well-shaft (Middle English *wynch*, Old English *wince*), and there seems little doubt that the well was named from the winding apparatus. In old Devon a *wink* was an apparatus used for spinning straw rope from reeds.

A *wink* in old Cornwall was also an alehouse. Beerhouses licensed by the excise authorities before the Beerhouse Act of 1869 were known as *tiddlywinks* in many parts of England, nobody knows why. But hence the Cornish and Devon adjective *tiddlywink*, drunk. *Tiddled* is an old slang word for drunk, and *to tiddle* to East Anglian and Warwickshire children means (or used to mean) to pee. Is there a connection? God only knows.

I came across a few more interesting wink-words while searching for the origin of Judy Ross's word. *Winky-pinky* is a Yorkshire nursery word for sleepy. *Winky-spinky* means puny, trifling, in Durham. *Winky-wanky* has been recorded in East Anglia; it means weak, pliant. *Wink-a-puss* is a Devon and Cornish word for an owl; it is also used as a term of contempt. *Wink-a-peep* is still used in Lancashire, Cheshire and Shropshire for the scarlet pimpernel, *Anagallis arvensis* to you botanists. The flower got its lovely dialect name from the fact that it opens to the morning sun and closes at noontide and at the approach of rain.

So that's it for now, except to tell those who wrote asking about the matter that I'm a man, and that my name is pronounced Deermid O Mwir-ih-heh, as near as dammit.

JUNE 1999

LIKE SHAKESPEARE'S Prince Henry I can boast that I can drink with any tinker in his own language. I have picked up a good deal of their secret language – known in Ireland and beyond as either Shelta, Sheldru or Minklas Thari (tinker talk) – from the ladies of a family who have camped on the outskirts of my village for many years back; they often come by to ask if I might boil a kettle for them, or to enquire if my daughter had any clothes she might give them in exchange for cheap rosaries or holy pictures. They are partial to a nip of whiskey as well as a cup of tea; but never once have they outstayed their welcome or taken advantage of an open door. In exchange for my goodwill they have taught me what they know of their Sheldru; it seems too that they have passed on a good word about me to their friends; mine is the only house in the neighbourhood that has not received unwelcome attention from them.

They are not gypsies and you dare not call them tinkers nowadays, or knackers either, though once they themselves were happy with the names. Knackers were very welcome in farmers' houses before the days of mechanized transport: they were saddle-makers and harness-menders and by plying their trade in the farmsteads they saved people long journeys to the towns where, as often as not, the only man who could mend a harness was a cobbler who wouldn't know a bog spavin from a running martingale. *Knacker* is from Old Norse *knackr*, a saddle.

The great Celtic scholar, Kuno Meyer, claimed that Sheldru was a relic of high antiquity, identical with the secret languages of the scholars and craftsmen of early Christian Ireland. Others have claimed that it is as old as the secret languages of the displaced druids. It is based on Irish, and its speakers used quite a lot of scholarly tricks to disguise it.

One was the reversal of syllables in an Irish word; the Irish *gunna*, a gun, became *nuga*, for example. Sometimes they reversed the whole word. This gave them *ad*, two, from Irish *dó* (pronounced doh); *kam*, son, from Irish *mac*; *luuk*, back, from Irish *cúl* (pronounced cool). They used apocope, the omission of the initial or final sound or sounds of a word, to good effect; their word *dooch*, clothes, is Irish *éadach* (say aydoch) with the first syllable discarded. Metathesis, the transposition of two sounds or letters in a word, also played a part. Examples are (the transposed letters are printed in capitals): *GoRed*, money, from Irish *aiRGead* (say arigad), *lurP*, flour, from *Plúr* (say ploor).

Here's a little sampler of Sheldru words. *Avali* (say awvally), a town; from Irish *baile* (say bolya), Hiberno-English *bally*. Another of their words for a town, *elum*, seems to be from the same source. *Been*, great; corrupted from Irish *mín* (say meen), fine. *Blinkam*, a candle: a factitious word this, from English *blink*. *Blorna*, a Protestant: uncertain origin. *Blantach*, a shirt: Irish *léine* (say layna). *Blewr*, a young woman: uncertain origin. *Bewr*, *beowr*, a woman: Irish *bean* (say ban); *bewr sreego*, a queen; *bewr swudal*, a lady. *Dura*, bread, from Irish *arán* (say arawn), reversed and de-nasalized. *Gasal*, a donkey, is from Irish *asal* (say ossul).

It has a few borrowings from languages other than Irish. *Forros*, a fair, is a Romany word borrowed from Greek. *Finnif*, a fiver, is a word of Yiddish origin.

Gifan is a horse, a distortion of Irish *capall* (say copul); *gloch*, *glok* is a man: this is probably Irish *óglach*, hero, in disguise. *Mwog* is a pig: Irish *muc*. *Mauso*, a dance, is from Irish *damhsa* (say dowsa). *Nadram*, mother. *Nadram tom*, grandmother; *nadram a Dhalyon*, mother of God, the Virgin Mary.

If you want more information, read *The Secret Languages of Ireland* by R.A. Stewart Macalister. The extensive glossary in this seminal book contains the collection of Paddy Greene, a schoolmaster from Ballinalee, Co. Longford, first published in 1935. We correspond frequently. He's indefatigable, and sure, why wouldn't he be? He won't be a hundred until this time next year. *Nus a Dhalyon dhuilsha*, as his friends would say: the blessing of God on you, oldie!

JULY 1999

CHARLES FITZGERALD of Andover wonders (May letters) whether I had got it right when I referred to the 'Anglo-Normans' of Co. Wexford. These men, he says, were Norman adventurers pure and simple, with nothing of the 'Anglo' about them, who spoke no English of any kind, rather Norman French. 'At any rate,' he goes on, 'they were mostly soon enough absorbed into the mainstream of Celtic Irish existence both in terms of marriage and native custom.'

True of everywhere else in Ireland except the place I was writing about, the baronies of Forth and Bargy on Wexford's south-east coast, a wedge of land no more than 12 miles from north to south and 15 from east to west. This place was settled by some of the adventurers and artisans who came with Fitzstephen, and it is simple historical fact that there were English, Welsh, Flemings and minor Norman nobility among them, and that their common language, coming as they did from 'little England beyond Wales', was a form of English.

It is evident from Stanihurst's *Description of Irelande* (1577) that by then the English of Forth differed widely from that of the court:

> There was of late dayes one of the Peeres of England sent to Weiseford as Commissioner ... and hearing in affable wise the rude complaintes of the countrey clownes, he conceyued here and there, sometyme a worde, other whyles a sentence. The noble man beyng very glad that upon his first commyng to Irelande he vnderstood so many wordes, told one of hys familiar frends that he stoode in very great hope to become shortly a well

spoken man in the Irishe, supposeing that the blunte people had pratled Irish, all the while they iangled Englishe.

As late as 1824 the Protestant rector of a Forth parish wrote that his workmen gave him better glosses on Chaucer than did the works of Dryden.

Far from being absorbed into the mainstream of Irish existence, they remained aloof from it. Towards the end of the 17th century Sir William Petty wrote: 'They seldom dispose of their children in marriage but unto natives, or such as will determine to reside in the barony.' They grew ashamed of the ways of their elders about a century and a half ago and abandoned Yola, their dialect, and many of their ancient customs, alas.

A hearty welcome to *The Mardler's Companion*, a splendid glossary of the dialect of East Anglia, compiled by Robert Malster and published by Malthouse Press. A *mardle* is defined thus: 'It can be used either as a verb, to gossip or chat, or as a noun. "We had a rare good ol' mardle, he and I."'

This engaging and accessible work should be required reading for Her Majesty's National Curriculum Council, if it still exists, a body which, a year or two back, was considering a purge of local dialect in schools, Mr Malster says.

It is a feast of folklore as well. Let me give you an example:

> *Bishabarnabee*: Dialect name for a ladybird, said to be a corruption of Bishop Bonner's bee. Bishop Bonner, whose home while rector of the parish is still to be seen at Dereham, having survived the fire which destroyed much of the town in 1581, has an unenviable reputation for having been responsible for the burning of several martyrs during the reign of Queen Mary. No doubt the fiery colour of the tiny beetle's wing cases led to its being given this local name. The German name for a ladybird is *Marienkäfer*, presumably in reference to the Virgin: it might be that the new reference to an unsavoury cleric was an attempt to replace a Roman Catholic name with a stoutly Protestant one. Children

used to chant the rhyme: *Ladybird, ladybird, fly away home, Your house is on fire, your children are gone.*

Lo and behold, we too have the East Anglian *mawkin*, a slut, in Wexford: 'a diminutive of Matilda or Maud, as early as the 14th century it was being used to describe a slatternly woman. Chaucer: "It wol not come agayn with outen drede Na moore than wol Malkynes maydenhede Whan she hath lost it in hir wantownesse."'

Wexford women were, of course, better behaved, but isn't it a small world?

AUGUST 1999

MANY OF THE LOVELY old wan words have faded away, and more's the pity. Some survive, thankfully. *Wan*, meaning black, and generally used of water, is still used in Scotland, Yorkshire and Warwickshire. 'Now did they swim that wan water' is a line from Scott's *Minstrelsy*. *Wan*, pale, sickly, has survived all over Britain, and *wan*, longing, wistful, is still heard in Cumbria. I think all those wans come from Old English *wann*, dark, dusky.

I once heard a Co. Antrim farmer describing a neighbour of his as 'a wan class of a wan'. His first wan meant that her figure was not as fully rounded, as plump as he liked 'em. His adjective is from Old English *wan*, wanting, deficient, lacking. His second wan is merely a local pronunciation of 'one'.

Another *wan*, this from Scotland, Shetland and Orkney, is a noun meaning success, hope, a prospect of success. From this they got *wanless*, hopeless, destitute. I once heard the Irish rugby team, then going through a lean spell, described by an Ulster follower as being as wanless as a cat in clabber (Irish *clábar*, mud). *Wanlie*, hopeful, auspicious, is from the same source, and has also survived. It has a pedigree going back to Old Norse *van*, hope, expectation. The extraordinary noun *wan*, meaning a direction, has also survived, it seems; so does its use as an adverbial affix. The *English Dialect Dictionary* helps out with this word. It explains that somebody coming from the Collieston wan, for example, means somebody coming from the Collieston direction.

Alas, the prefix *wan*, signifying want or wane, seems to have disappeared, as far as I know. Isn't *wanhope*, despair, a lovely word? Ivor Brown, who worked with the *Observer* long ago, thought that the added notion of wanness in colour as well as of waning gave special poignance to the word. Both Chaucer and my Wexford granny had it. The former had 'Well ought I sterve in wanhope and distresse' in *The Canterbury Tales*; I was the wanhope of the latter.

Wanluck has disappeared from Scotland. It meant misfortune. Gone too is *wangrace*, which seems such a gentle word for wickedness, and *wanwit*, foolishness. This Middle English word has relatives in Modern Swedish *vanvett*, in Danish *vanvid* and in German *wahnwitz*.

I wonder does the marvellous *wanwauchtie* survive in Scotland? It means unable to take a lot of drink. Burns has made *waucht* famous the world over with his *guid-willie waucht*, the dram of kindliness. There's a Scots proverb, 'He's unco wanwauchtie that scunners at whey.' *Scunners* means dislikes, shrinks away from.

Some queries. M. Singleton from Norwich asks me where the verb *to yag* originates. To him it means to squabble. There are various shades of meaning: to make a noise, to talk angrily, to irritate. All these were recorded in Scotland, and I have no idea where they originated. Mr Singleton's word is easily traceable – it's from Old Norse *jag*, a quarrel. Vigfusson's dictionary, the last word on these matters, has *jagast*, to altercate.

Joyce Prince sent me the Somerset word *nestletripe*, 'the runt of the sow's litter; the tiny little thing who is too feeble to fight the siblings for food'. There are many variants, *nestledraught*, *-draft*, or *-draff* from Devon; and in the case of both birds and humans, *nestlecock*, *nestlebird*, *nestlebub* and *nestledris* were also recorded in the south-east.

Middleton has nestlecock in *Anything for a Quiet Life* in 1626: 'My mother was wont to call me your nestlecock, and I love you as well as she did.' The *EDD* gives *nestling* and *nesslin* as both the smallest and weakest bird in the nest, from Scotland and, from Somerset, the smallest pig of the litter. The *nestle* bit is from Old English *nestlian*, but as for the second element in Joyce's word, her guess is as good as mine.

R.S. Smylie from York tells me that when he was young, naughty children used to shout, 'Nicker, nicker!' at large ladies. It used to annoy them greatly, he says. They would be even more annoyed if they knew that the word came from Old English *nicor*, a hippopotamus. Had they any words for wan wans, I wonder?

SEPTEMBER 1999

I AM CURRENTLY engaged in a skirmish with the *Oxford English Dictionary* and shortly, I feel, I shall be having it out with the estimable Robert Malster, compiler and editor of the splendid *The Mardler's Companion*, a dictionary of East Anglian dialect, mentioned in this column recently.

This is my problem. You will remember Hamlet's bit of crack with Guildenstern: 'I am but mad north-north-west; when the wind is southerly I know a hawk from a handsaw.' *Oxford* seems to think that *handsaw* is a form of *heronshaw*, and Mr Malster goes further. Let me quote him:

> In 1776 Pennant wrote that 'Not to know the Hawk from the Heronshaw was an old proverb taken from this diversion [heronhawking]; but in course of time served to express great ignorance in any science.' Forby spells the word *harnsey*, but remembering the Norfolk habit of changing a *y* sound into an *a* ... it is perhaps better spelt as we have done [*harnser*]. It is in origin not a dialect word at all but a contraction of the old word *heronsew* or *heronshaw*, a diminutive of heron.

All right, a heron was the prey of the hawk, which was considered a destroyer of fish stocks. But the leap from heronshaw to handsaw (or indeed harnser) is too much for me. I recently had a letter from Eoin Ó Cofaigh, President of the Royal Institute of the Architects of Ireland, which confirmed my suspicions. A *hawk*, he pointed out, was, and has been for centuries past, a plasterer's name for a mortarboard, the flat board with a handle underneath. This was the hawk Hamlet was referring to, we both think, and Shakespeare had nothing more in mind in 'hawk' and 'handsaw' than two common tradesmen's tools.

How old is this word hawk for a plasterer's mortarboard? It was first mentioned in a word-list of tradesmen's terms in 1700, *Oxford* says. Considering the conservatism of tradesmen's speech, considering that the term is still in use among them, would they not acknowledge that this hawk was first attested to in Shakespeare? No. Hamlet's hawks and handsaws were probably birds, they say. Ah well. I have long since given up hope that they will accept my contention that the English *pet*, which they say is of uncertain origin, is from the Old Irish *peta*, or *petta*, a tame or domesticated animal. Years ago I recommended that they read an article in the learned journal *Revue Celtique* (xliv) for their further enlightenment. They didn't reply.

Here's a reply to Ann James of Oldham who wants to know something of the word *bree*, soup, broth, gravy. The word is still common in both Scotland and Ulster, and also in parts of Yorkshire and Lancashire. A wonderful old Donegal lady, Grace O'Boyle, who now resides in Leicester and who will sip a glass of champagne on New Year's Day next to commemorate the fact that she will then have lived in three centuries, once told me that in the hard times she grew up in, *bree* also meant the water the supper potatoes were boiled in. This was never thrown out before the children washed their feet in it. From Middle English *bre* this. The *Liber Cocorum* of *c.* 1420 speaks of 'fat bre fresshe of befe'.

Pamela Craig of Kelvinside, Glasgow, writes:

> I hope this query won't embarrass you, but I recently heard some young ladies who considered themselves well-bred use a certain word when speaking disparagingly about friends who have had, I feel, rather more success with the boys than they have had. On enquiring what exactly sentences such as 'That one has nothing but *colfing* on her mind' mean, I have been greeted with a snigger. Can you explain what exactly they have in mind?

To colf, dear Pamela, means to stuff. It was a word once commonly used by both soldiers and sailors. To colf a gun meant to wad it, and to colf a ship meant to caulk her, as the great Cotgrave in his 17th-century dictionary explains: 'French, *calfater*, to caulk a ship, to stop or fill the rifts thereof with ockam'. John Florio, sometimes accused of colfing James I's queen, Anne of Denmark, has *calafate*, a caulker, in his engaging Italian-English dictionary. Good for the well-bred lasses of Kelvinside for making the word their own!

OCTOBER 1999

PAULINE BROWN wrote to me some time ago from Buckstone Road, Edinburgh, asking about a word which, she says, is common in Lincolnshire: *crew-yard*, a farm-yard.

The word *crew* is found in the dialects of Ireland as *crew* and *crow*, in Scotland as *crue* and *craw*; in Wales as *crau*; in Lancashire, Cheshire, Devon and Cornwall as *crow*. *Crew* is also found in Shetland and Orkney. A crew-yard can also mean a fold for sheep, in the English Midlands, and also a yard in which the hay-lofts and corn-lofts are situated. A *crew* is a coop for hens and ducks in Yorkshire and Cheshire, and a pigsty, hut or hovel in both the highlands of Scotland and Ulster.

The word's origin is Celtic, and at least two strains of Celtic have had an influence here. There is the earlier Welsh *creu* (*crau*), and you may compare *crewyn*, *crowen*, sty, pen, hovel; include in this group the Old Cornish, which has *crow*, a pigsty, a hovel, and its close relative, the Breton *kraou*. From the second Celtic family we have the Irish *cró*, in Hiberno-English as *crow*, a hovel, a pigsty, a fowl-house, a fold, which gave Scots Gaelic its word, *cró*, which has identical meanings. The Welsh/Cornish/Breton group was, I suppose, the influence that led to the formation of the Lincolnshire dialect word.

Where I come from, a sovereign remedy for the chin-cough was to pass the afflicted child three times under the belly of an ass. The *chin-cough* was the whooping cough, and the word was once common all over Britain. Jane Coles from Chester wrote to ask about the word's origin, and if you think we Wexfordians were slightly odd in believing in the strange curative property of an ass's undercarriage, listen to what Jane heard in her native place:

> Every woman who retained her name when she got married had the cure for the chin-cough, which, in the days before inoculation, could be a serious matter. Another remedy was to make the children eat either a hedgehog or a mouse; fried or boiled, it didn't matter. The mountain ash also had magical properties. A lock of the child's hair was tied to the tree, and the fairies worked their charms.

There is a whole chapter on England's folk-cures in the 1883 edition of the journal *Folk-Lore*, and from it, here is another infallible remedy for the chin-cough (sometimes written *chink-cough*):

> At Whittington the remedy is to pass the child three times under and three times over a briar which simply grows out from the hedge, saying meanwhile, 'Over the briar and under the briar, and out goes the chin-cough.' Usually a briar of which the root grows in one parish while the end hangs over into another is prescribed. If the further end has rooted, so much the better. At Market

Drayton, which stands close to the boundaries of Shropshire, Staffordshire and Cheshire, a bramble which grows in three counties is required.

But I digress. Why chin-cough? was Jane's question. Chin-cough was a variant of *kink-cough*, another dialect word for whooping-cough. In Simmon's 1890 glossary of south Donegal English we find: 'I know a spring well known as the kink-well, because it has the reputation of curing chin-cough.' This *kink* is our clue to the word's origin. The word is Teutonic; the Low German has *kinkhoost* for whooping cough.

T.C. Jefferies from Durham tells me that the word *beck* is found in sixty-three place-names in that county. I'd well believe it; you'll find it wherever the Vikings left their mark in England. Yorkshire has a lot of becks; so have Lincolnshire, Norfolk, Suffolk and Sussex. There are no becks in Ireland, as far as I know. Howitt's *Rural England* (1838) says of Yorkshire: 'The smaller streams are called sykes, the larger gills, and the largest, being generally those which run along the dale, becks.' (*Syke* is from Old English *sic*, a watercourse, a runnel, incidentally; *gill* from Old Norse *gil*, a steep glen with a stream at its bottom.)

The *English Dialect Dictionary* quotes an amusing epitaph for the Rev. John Becke, rector of Kettlethorpe in Lincolnshire, who died in 1597: 'I am a Becke, or river as you know, And wat'red here ye Church, ye schole, ye pore.'

The Old Norse is *bekkr*, a brook.

NOVEMBER 1999

As I sat down to write this the phone rang, and a worried friend from New York told me that there is a nasty little mosquito going the rounds, doing serious damage to the health of the

Manhattan populace, causing encephalitis among other things. 'Are there any precautions I could take?' I asked, for I was departing for a holiday there in the morning. 'None,' I was told, 'but the Mayor, who is being blamed in some quarters for the mosquitoes' capers, is having the city sprayed with chemicals every night, so you should survive.' Let us hope so.

The Scots of the Western Isles had an antidote for plagues of all kinds, but as I can find no mention of mosquitoes in the literature about the *Tin-Egin*, I decided not to resort to it that night. In 1716 Martin Martin, a traveller to the Isles, had this to say:

> The inhabitants here did also make use of a fire called *Tin-Egin*, ie a forced fire, or fire of necessity, which they used as an antidote against disasters such as the plague, and it was performed thus: All the fires in the parish were extinguished and then eighty-one married men, being thought the necessary number for affecting the design, took two great planks of wood, and nine of 'em were employed in turns, who by their repeated efforts rubbed one of the planks against the other until the heat thereof produced fire; and from this forc'd fire each family is supply'd with new fire, which is no sooner kindled than a pot full of water is quickly set on it and afterwards sprinkled upon the people infected with the plague. And this they all say they find successful by experience.

Tin-Egin is, as the man said, forced fire; *teine* is the Gaelic for fire; *eiginn*, violence. A relic of Druidic religion, this. I find the sprinkling of the water intriguing. No doubt Alice Thomas Ellis can tell me if the Holy Water of Christian churches has its origins in the mysterious Celtic past.

George Hand from Pembroke wrote about a phrase common in his young days, one which, he says,

> you might hear uttered by the coarser kind of young fellows when they referred to young maidens of demure and chaste

demeanour, for which Pembrokeshire is justly famous: 'God, try as I might, but I couldn't even knock a vonk out of her.'

George, with commendable delicacy, says that he hopes that vonk is not a word that would cause me to blush.

Vonk wouldn't cause even the girls mentioned above to blush. It means a spark, and is either from Middle Dutch *vonck*, a sparkle, or Middle High German *vanke*, a spark. It is related to the East Anglian and Hampshire words for a spark, *funk*. Compare the German *funke*.

Speaking of the sparks of love, *selemnic* was a word used by William Barnes, the Dorset dialect poet and scholar of the last century. I think he made the word, and if so, good for him. It means 'in a state of oblivion'. The late Bedell Stanford, great classical scholar and, for his sins, my tutor in Dublin's Trinity College, traced the word's existence, made up by Barnes or not, to a delightful story told by Pausanias in the 2nd century AD. It is set in the Northern Peloponnese:

> Selemnos was a beautiful shepherd boy and Argyra was a lovely sea-nymph who fell in love with him. They say that she used to come from the sea to visit him and to sleep with him. But time took its toll on the mortal shepherd boy, and the sea-nymph would visit him no more. So he lost his Argyra and pined away, and died of love. But Aphrodite pitied him and gave him immortality by turning him into a river. Even then he pined for her; so Aphrodite bestowed on him a priceless favour: Selemnos forgot his Argyra completely. And I've heard it said that the waters of Selemnos are equally good for a man or woman to cure the wounds of love, and if you wash in that river you'll forget the hurt and the pain that attend a broken love affair. If there is truth in this, the water of Selemnos is worth more to mankind that all the money in the world.

Amen.

DECEMBER 1999

'OUR DOOR NEVER KEELS at Christmas; we have visitors from all over, not to mention friendly neighbours coming in for a cup of tea and a chat.' So wrote Jennifer Lowe of Barnsley to me. She wonders if I've come across the verb *to keel*, which means to cool, in my travels.

Indeed I have, but I've never heard it applied to a busy house. When greasy Joan keeled the pot in *Love's Labour's Lost*, what she was doing was cooling it, keeping it from boiling over either by stirring, taking it off the fire, or by skimming a ladleful and exposing it to the air. To skim is what Wycliff meant in *Piers Plowman* when he wrote 'to kele a crockke, and chill'; in his translation of St Luke he has, 'Sende Lazarus, that he dippe the ende of his fyngur in watir, to kele my tunge.'

Keel is from Old English *celan*, to cool, to make cold. Well done, Yorkshire, for preserving the word in Jennifer's figurative sense.

Cathy Barrington is a Lincolnshire woman who had the good sense in her youth to marry a Wexfordman. At Christmas, she tells me, her mother used to make *haslets*, and she tells me that these thick puddings, a favourite Lincolnshire dish, are delicious. I'll take her word for it. Haslets are made from minced pork, sage and onions; the mixture is baked in the pig's caul. 'A good hog's harslet, a piece of meat I love!' wrote an unusually contented Pepys in 1664. But Mrs Barrington's reason for writing was not to proclaim the wonders of Lincolnshire Christmas cuisine, but to ask where the word came from.

Gawayne and the Green Knight (c. 1360) refers to these sausages as *hastlettez*. They may have been French originally: *hastelet* was the Old French word for roast meat, a diminutive of *haste*, a spit, which gave its name to the meat cooked on it. The origin of this *haste* was the Latin *hasta*, a spear.

Cathy's mention of mince reminds me that the word also has a Latin origin in *minutus*, small, and *minutia*, smallness, words that trickled in Old French as *menuisier*, which gave the Normans *mincier*, which gave Middle English *mynce*. In her letter she mentioned a gravy used as a condiment with the haslet, but gives no details. *Gravy*, too, is a French import, it seems. *Oxford* explains that the Middle English may have misread a word in the Old French cookery books, of which they became very fond. The word in question was *grané*, a spicy sauce used in the preparation of fish. This word's probable origin is Old French *grain*, grain, from the grains of various Middle Eastern spices used in the condiment. This was printed in the English books as *grauey, gravey*, and *gravé*, and the form quickly became current and permanent as a term in English cooking.

What a dull Christmas table we must have had before the Crusades. No turkeys, no guinea fowl; no raisins, almonds, figs or dates to fill our sweet pies. The following recipe quoted by *Oxford* from *Two Cookery Books*, written in the middle of the 15th century, would, I fancy, still go down a treat: it is for trayne roste (a *trayn* [train] was a dish consisting of dates, figs, raisins and almonds hung upon a long thread and covered with batter):

> Take dates and figges ... and then take grete reysons and blanched almondes, and prik them throgh with a nedel into the threde of a mannys length ... rost the treyne abought the fire in the spete; cast the batur on the treyne as he turneth abought the fire.

Raisin is a borrowing from the Old French *raizin*, from the Provençal *razin*, from Latin *racemum*. When the English borrowed the word in the 13th century they generally referred to it as *raisin sec*, a sun-dried grape. *Dates* came from Old French *date*, from Latin *dactylus*, from the Greek *daktulos*, a finger, which they thought it resembled; *fig* is from Old French *figue*, from Latin *ficus*; and *almond* came from French *almande*, earlier *alemandre*, through Latin *amygdala*, from the Greek *amugdale*.

May I just wish you full and plenty this Christmas, and the health to enjoy it. Sláinte!

JANUARY 2000

IN THE MOUNTAINOUS county of Wicklow, the garden of Ireland, where I live, January is the time of year in which you'll be likely to see venison dishes served in even the poorest of country cottages. In January the deer come down from the mountains into the woods and valleys to escape the winter snows, and this leads to a certain amount of illegal culling. So, instead of a diet of Carthusian simplicity after the excesses of Christmas, we eat humble pie, which is, in my humble opinion, far more palatable than the venison steaks of the expensive restaurants.

Humble pie, used nowadays only in a figurative sense, has nothing to do with humility, although it was, indeed, a pie eaten by humble people in the bad old days. When the Normans ruled these islands the barons would eat the better cuts of venison, while the serfs were given the rest, what the cookery books call the edible viscera, the liver, heart and kidneys; and the chine and other cuts not considered prime. The Normans called these *nombles*, plural of *nomble*, thigh muscle, a word they got by making a hash of the Latin *lumbulus*, a slice of meat, from *lumbus*, loin. By Chaucer's time nombles had slipped into English as *numbles*; by the 15th century it had become *umbles*, and by the 16th, *humbles*. By Shakespeare's time the lord of the manor was still eating his roast of prime venison, while the lesser mortals were content with the shoulder and the edible viscera cooked in a crusted pie, *umble pie*.

This was the more common spelling until our own day. Pepys in his diary of 8 July 1663 has: 'Mrs Turner came in, and did bring us an umble pie hot out of her oven, extraordinary good.' Nothing socially inferior in this; the man obviously relished his dish of venison. Dickens spelt it *umble* in *David Copperfield*; indeed it wasn't until the 20th century that the spelling humble pie became universal, and given a figurative meaning for the first time.

I was described recently in a rural Irish newspaper as 'a scavenger in the dump of words'. Ouch! I would have described my trade more poetically, quoting Chaucer: '... wel I woot that folk han here-beforn Ropen, and lad away the corn; And I am come after, glenynge here and there, And am ful glad if I may fynde an ere Of any goodly word that they han left.' The columnist in question was being complimentary, believe it or not; he was musing on the word scrum, in anticipation of Ireland's winning the wooden spoon in the forthcoming Five Nations tournament, and told his readers that he would ask me about the word's origin.

Scrum came either from *scrimmage* or *scrimish*, 15th-century variants of *skirmish*. In the 18th century *scrimmage* came to mean a noisy brawl. Rugby football borrowed it and shortened it to scrum. *Skirmish* is from Middle English *skyrmissh*, itself from one or other of two older Middle English nouns, *skarmish*, *scarmuch*; the alteration is due to the influence of the Middle English verb *skirmysshen*, to engage in swordplay. *Skarmish* and *skarmuch* are from Middle French *escarmouche*, which, like the Old Italian *scaramuccia*, also meaning skirmish, can be traced to Old High German *skirmen*, to defend.

Scaramuccia became a stock character in Italian farce, and was meant to represent a Spanish nobleman, a blustering coward: a bit of ethnic humour not appreciated south of the Pyrenees. *Scaramouch* became a common word in English after the success of a play of that name by Edward Ravenscroft in 1677. A long, winding road, with many byways, from the German defensive swordplay to the rugby scrum.

As to *scavenger*, in 14th-century England many towns levied a tax called *scavage* on goods sold by non-residents. The word is from Old French *escauwage*, inspection, and is related, through a common Germanic ancestor, to a similar Anglo-Saxon levy, *sceawung*, which meant 'showing'. The scavagers, who later picked up an intrusive 'n' in their trade description, collected the scavage, but they also had to keep the streets clean. When their original job was forgotten they remained street cleaners; now a scavenger is a collector of junk from council dumps. Or, it would seem, a lexicographer.

FEBRUARY 2000

ONE OF THE PLEASURES of working in the world of lexicography is the chance of finding words deemed dead and consigned to history by the great dictionaries. Such a word came my way recently in a letter from Helen North of Canterbury. In her china cabinet rests her father's *tygo*, an earthenware drinking utensil with three handles. Helen tells me that a lot of the old-timers she once knew had the word, and that even in recent times she has heard oldies speak of 'going for a tygo' on a Saturday night.

As to the word's origin, it is a form of *tyg* or *tig*, once common in Staffordshire, Yorkshire and in some of England's southern counties. Where this word comes from is a mystery to *Oxford*; more about that later. *Notes and Queries* for 1891, seventh series, tells us that in Staffordshire the potters of 1801 called their cups and porringers *tigs*, and that the tig, more correctly *tyg*, was made in the Staffordshire potteries in large quantities in the 17th and 18th centuries. The same learned journal elsewhere informs us that 'there was in use at Cambridge, about the beginning of the 17th century, a three-handled silver cup containing about a quart. The handles were equidistant from one another, and the cup was called a tig.'

Why, you might ask, were there three handles? In de la Beche and Reeks, *Catalogue of Specimens of British Pottery* (1855), we are told that 'The tyg was so handled that three different persons, drinking out of it, and each using a separate handle, bring their mouths to different parts of the rim.' The *English Dialect Dictionary* quotes *Wakefield Words*, compiled in 1865: 'Tyg, verb. In phrase *as full as he can tyg*, said of anyone who has drunk as much ale as he can.'

As to the origin of the word, *Oxford* says that it is of uncertain pedigree. It quotes an old Anglo-Saxon dictionary that asks us to consider *tigel*. But that would give modern *tile*. No. I suggest that the word's origin is Old English *tyge*, a draught of water, which gave the compound *tygehorn*, a drinking vessel.

'I'm arranty tired of your behaviour,' Judith Constable's mother, a Lancashire woman, used to complain whenever the daughter got up to some *andramartins* (Hiberno-English, meaning nonsensical tricks, origin unknown). *Arrant*, meaning entirely, thoroughly, downright, usually in a bad sense, is old. 'The moon's an arrant thief,' wrote Shakespeare in *Timon of Athens*; 'We are arrant thieves, all,' he decided in *Hamlet*. The word is in English since before 1400. The original meaning was wandering, vagabond, from the French *errant*, present participle of *errer*.

Three people wrote asking about the word *latchico*, an arrant boyo, a scoundrel. One is a lady who works at the BBC in Belfast and who doesn't want to be named; the second is James Glover from Birmingham; and the third is Henrietta Hunter from Coventry.

The word was once confined to Irish labourers from the west of Ireland who worked on English building sites; I'm told that it has now spread far and wide in the English Midlands. One theory is that the word is from Old French *laschier*, relax. A recent book says that 'it has been suggested that latch represents children who have to let themselves in by the latch and thus become delinquent as time goes by'. Oh dear.

The word is an anglicization of the Irish compound *leath-tiochóg*, pronounced in western Irish as *latchico*, with these minor differences, that the final *g* in the Irish word became redundant, and that the final *c* in the Irish is aspirate and pronounced like the *ch* in Scots *loch*. *Leath*, pronounced like the *la* in latchico, means half, and is used exactly as was *healfh* in Old English compounds such as *healfhwit*. *Tioch*, diminutive *tiochóg*, means a bag, and figuratively a scrotum; when the Mayo labourers, who were only one generation removed from being native speakers of Irish, called someone a latchico, what they had in mind was a half-bollocks, if you'll pardon the crudity.

MARCH 2000

MARGARET MILLER wrote to me from Leeds in the middle of drear January. She had been looking out at an old ash tree she has at the bottom of her garden, stripped of its leaves, cradling no birds now. In her youth, in common with many of her friends, she used to climb that tree when it came into leaf, searching for even ash. She went on to explain that it was as lucky to find even ash as it was to find a four-leafed clover; girls would wear a little sprig of it for luck, and would put it in the left shoe, however uncomfortable that might be, to ensure that a sweetheart would come their way before long.

Even ash is an ash-leaf with an even number of leaflets, and in Antrim's glens it is still used as a means of divination. 'The young girl who finds one', wrote the Ulster lexicographer, W.H. Patterson, 'repeats the words, "This even ash I hold in my han'; The first I meet is my true man."' Patterson was one of Wright's most important contributors to his *English Dialect Dictionary*; neither was surprised when lore about the divination properties of even ash was sent in from many places in England. From Wiltshire, Wright was sent the news that on King Charles's Day, 29 May, children collect *shitsack* (*shit* being the Wiltshire past participle of *shut*), sprigs of young oak, in the morning, and even ash in the evening. From Yorkshire, a farmer explained that *ash-keys* were the seed vessels of the ash, and that there were no ash-keys in the year in which King Charles was put to death. Wright records that in Northampton 'a superstition prevails that some member of the royal family will die within the year if there is a scarcity of ash-keys'.

Ash-key is old. You'll find it as *esch key* in *Promptorium Parvulorum Sive Clericorum*, an Anglo-Latin lexicon of about 1440, republished by the Camden Society, and often consulted by harmless old drudges like myself. Ash is from Old English *oesc*, cognate with Old Norse *askr*, Middle High German *asch* and Modern German *esche*. Key, in the sense I've mentioned, is found all over Scotland and England. Is it, in this sense, related to the key with which things are locked up, from Old English *coeg*, I wonder?

Alice Nesbitt wrote to me from Manchester recently about an interesting word she spells *bysen*. The word means a ridiculous spectacle. It is still in use in northern England. In Yorkshire, back in the time when the pulpit ruled, a common expression, referring to a tawdrily dressed woman, was 'What a holy bysen!', and the allusion was explained in one of the glossaries as 'probably pointing to the custom, practised within the memory of living men in some of our Dale churches, of setting offenders against morality, supposed or required to be penitents, arrayed in white sheets, on the Stool of Repentance during the hours of divine service'. Origin? Compare the Old Norse *bysn*, a wondrous thing, and the Old English *bysen*, an example.

No doubt *kittling* was an offence that could have led to the Stool of Repentance in the good old days. This old word was used recently in my Wicklow local by a young lady on holidays from Kent. It means to get a man all excited, confided the lass, who was flirting outrageously with a local footballer who fancies himself, but whose value on the transfer market would be around a fiver. Such was their ardour that I thought it unlikely that they'd be interested in an interpolation from me, to the effect that this *kittle* comes from the Old English verb *citelian*, to tickle.

When I say her ladyship's boyfriend was *simpering* at her bonhomie, I use that verb as they still do in Antrim and in west Yorkshire: in the sense to simmer. Palsgrave's French-English lexicon of 1530 has simper in this sense: 'I symper as lycour dothe on the fyre before it begynneth to boyle.'

'We're leaving,' said the boyfriend suddenly. He stalked out into the Wicklow night. And up she got and followed him without a word to the next Roy Keane. It's a long swim from here to England, after all.

APRIL 2000

ON A FLIGHT from Dublin to a continental destination not so long ago, I had a word with the captain, who was doing a goodwill tour of the plane. I asked him whether it would be possible for a girl who was sitting near me to see the cockpit, and he graciously invited her up. He told her to tell one of the stewardesses to escort her just as soon as he got back there. This I did for her. I got a glare in reply.

Ten minutes later I asked another stewardess, got another baleful glance and, once again, no reply. Ten minutes later I asked yet another green-clad colleen, and got the same treatment. An old lady sitting near me asked for a glass of water and was told that she should have asked for it when they were giving out the drinks. They did, eventually, bring it to her.

I expressed my disappointment that a once model airline had descended to these standards. 'We're busy,' explained Stewardess One. Living up to my Christian name, which means peaceful, without rancour, I said no more. The old lady who needed water muttered about a shower of carlings.

A good word this *carling*; I'm told that you can hear it still in England's North Country and in some of the southern dialects. It's from Old Norse. *Kerling* was their word for a quarrelsome woman,

nearly always an old woman, according to Vigfusson, whose great dictionary Oxford University Press has allowed to go out of print. The Scots and the Ulster people have retained carling, too. Rab Burns refers to 'shakin' hands wi' wabster loons and kissing barefit carlins' in his *Epistle to Graham*.

I see that the bould Rab also had the word *cleckin*, a brood of chickens, figuratively a large family; this was sent to me by Mrs Judith Harmon from Newcastle. Cleckin is also an import from Scandinavia. It is also found in the English of Ulster; my wife, God rest her, who was from Co. Donegal, used it. Burns, in his *Verses to Creech*, has,

> He cleeps like some bewildered chicken
> Scared frae its minnie and the cleckin by hoodie-craw.

Mrs Harmon has unwittingly caused a last-minute hitch in the republication, in paperback, of a dictionary I once wrote of words and phrases that have entered the English of Ireland from Irish. At any rate, I, forever railing at people who fall for folk-etymologies, have the phrase *on the batter*, on a spree, as being from Irish *ar an mbóthar*, which translates as 'on the road', on a pub-crawl, so to speak.

Oh, dear me! Mrs Harmon tells me that the phrase originated among English building workers, and to them *on the batter* means anything that is tottering or askew. So, the meaning 'on a spree' is secondary.

The good lady also pointed to the verb *to batter*. I reached for my *English Dialect Dictionary*. There it is: 'To build a wall, ditch, embankment, out of the perpendicular. Of a wall: to incline, to taper.' From Cheshire: 'In building a wall, particularly against a bank, the term batter is used, and means to make the wall inclined so as to withstand by its inclination the pressure of the earth, which, were the wall not battered, would bring it down.' I see that Ash's lexicon of 1795 has 'Batter (used only by artificers), to lean from the perpendicular.' Well, we live and learn.

At least I can help Jean Cross from York with the adjective *chollous*, nasty, irritable. It comes from Middle English *cherlous*, related to modern *churlish* and applicable to women as well as to men. *Vide supra*.

MAY 2000

LONG BEFORE my time a cat was known in my south-east corner of Ireland as *baudrons*. The *English Dialect Dictionary* found the word only in Scotland and in England's border counties, which surprises me; I've heard it myself in Antrim, and in the form *badrons* in Devon. Beryl Hume from Ayr has the word; she wants to know where it comes from.

It has a Celtic origin, I'd say, although it's hard to be absolutely certain about this. There's the Irish adjective *beadrach*, pronounced something like badrock, gamesome, frolicsome; and the Scots Gaelic noun *beadrach*, a playful girl; a fondling, a caressing as well. That great Ayrman, Robert Burns, has 'Just like a winkit baudrons' in *Ordination*, written in 1786. I'm glad to hear the word survives up there.

In the south-east of Ireland a tomcat, and, figuratively, a man who behaves like one, is called a *boldoon*. It has been suggested that this word is somehow etymologically related to baudrons, and perhaps it is. Another theory is that the word may have originated in some long-forgotten Anglo-Norman *Baldwin*, who happened to be, in Sean O'Faolain's phrase, a bit weak in the carnalities. He must have been very weak in them to have been known in four counties. No. I'll stick with the randy cat theory.

I've come across some good cat compounds. My son, a medicine man, once sent me the dialect word *catterels* from Lancashire. This is an eruptive skin disorder and so named because it looks like the scratches of a cat. This comes by way of Scots and Northern English *arr*, sometimes *err*, a blemish, a scar, from Old Norse *orr*.

Richard Rolle de Hampole, writing in Northumberland around 1340, complained: 'Thei ere brokyn myn erres', which he translated in case you thought he didn't know his erres from his elbow: 'Corruptae sunt cicatrices meae.'

Cat-blash is from Lincolnshire. It means very weak tea or overbaptized whisky. It also has the figurative meaning, foolish talk. Blash, like splash, is onomatopaeic, and its primary meaning here is pee. *Cat's hair* is used in Perthshire for the downy hair on an adolescent boy's face. Girls use it to tease young fellows, I'm told. It also means cirrus and cirrus-stratus clouds, which look somewhat like hairs streaming from a cat's tail. *Cat's clipping* in Yorkshire was, and perhaps still is, the tea-drinking that took place when a baby was born. I have no idea how this one originated. If clip here means Shakespeare's and Chaucer's embrace, as has been suggested, what has the wretched cat to do with it?

Cat's-lick is still in general use for a perfunctory washing or grooming. The Norfolk *cat's arse* is a prissy woman; in Cornwall it is a mean, tight-fisted woman. *Cat-ice* is thin ice. John Clare has 'the cat-ice chatters where the schoolboy passed' in one of his poems. *Cat-witted* in Cumberland means dissolute and untrustworthy. The poet Hogg spelled this *cat-wuddied*: 'What ails the owld cat-wuddied carle?'

The poor old baudrons is mentioned in dispatches by gardeners all over Britain and Ireland. *Cat's love* is the garden valerian in west Yorkshire; cats like to roll in it, apparently. In my part of Ireland *cat's love* is cultivated heather. *Cats-and-dogs* are the catkins of the willow, a substitute for palm on Palm Sunday in Cornwall; *cat's paws* in Wiltshire. *Cat posy* is the common daisy in Cumbria; and in Northumberland *cat's foot* is the ground ivy.

The folklore journals are full of lore about cats. Full of interesting phrases, too. 'To live under the sign of the cat's foot' was to be henpecked in Yorkshire, according to *Ray's Proverbs* of 1678. 'I wish I had our own cat by the tail,' was said by Yorkshire people when they were far from home and lonely. 'To nurse the cat' was to be idle in Suffolk. 'To shoot the cat' was to be sick from drink in

Hampshire. Sailors had a saying, 'The cat has a gale of wind in her tale.' That marvellous book, *Swainson's Weather Folk-Lore*, published in 1873, explains the saying: 'Sailors have a great dislike to see a cat, aboard ship, being usually playful and frolicsome: such an event, they consider, prognosticates a storm.'

Which takes us a long way from Beryl Hume's question. Blame her.

JUNE 2000

PATRICIA FLEMING of Chepstow, in the course of a charming letter, tells me that she is from Yorkshire and was sent to Scarborough Girls' High School, where many of the pupils were farmers' daughters from 'up on t'moors', and had very broad accents. The school employed an English teacher from darn sarth (Surrey), who made the girls say such sentences as, 'The butcher sat on a cushion neath a bush when his wife called, "Come and cut the bread and butter." ' The object of this exercise was to stop the girls from the moors saying 'coome' and 'booter'. But their pride in Yorkshire English was restored when a headmaster from another school gave them a talk on the origins of their dialect, encouraging the use of such phrases as *lahrtle bairn*, little child.

I was wondering about the word *rov*, which I heard in the south-west of Ireland some years ago, in a district where the Irish language was still spoken only a generation ago. The spelling is mine; I've never seen the word in print. It means a saw. Patricia has never heard the noun rov used, but she points to dialect verb to rive. In *Yorkshire*, by Richard Blakeborough (1898), she found, 'Ah s'all rive t'maist o' yon wood up,' which means 'I shall split up most of the wood over there.' She thinks that my rov comes from rive, which survives in the Standard English past participle *riven*.

Rive is from Old Norse *rifa*, to rub, grate, rasp, etc., according to *Oxford*; Patricia would be inclined to place 'to saw' among the et ceteras. Such a transference is, indeed, possible.

Her suggestion sent me to the Old Norse dictionaries, where I found another Old Norse verb: *raufa*, to rip open, to tear. Vigfusson's dictionary has *raufa brjóst*, to cut the breast open. Could raufa be the ancestor of rov? Is rifa etymologically related to raufa, with some common Teutonic ancestor?

Well, unless somebody comes up with a better solution, rov will go into my forthcoming dictionary of words that have entered the English of Ireland from languages other than Irish, with the note saying, 'probably of Norse origin', and asking the reader to compare rifa and raufa, with acknowledgments to Patricia and Steve.

Keith Barnes of Bournemouth has sent me some fascinating words from Norfolk. These were published in *The Land of the Broads*, by E.R. Suffling in 1893. I wonder are they still in use? A *cob* is a Norfolk seagull. It is also a male swan. Coles in his 1679 dictionary has 'a cob-swan, *cygnus olor*'. *Dannocks* are hedging gloves. Suffling doesn't give etymologies; dannock is from *Dorneck*, the Flemish name for Tournai, where they were made from strong, pliable leather.

A *gotch* is a large jug or pitcher. I have no idea where this came from. *Grissons* are Norfolk stairs. Marshall has the word in his *Rural Economy* (1787), but the word is far older. Maundeville has it in his *Voiage* of 1400: 'thei maken ther of grecynges and pileres and pawmentes'. Its origin is the Old French *grez*, plural of *gré*, taken as a collective singular in the sense flight of steps, staircase. This gave English *grece* around 1300. *Cursor Mundi* from that date has: 'a grece ther was of steppis fijftene'.

To hain means to raise – either the rent, or the stack, or a building, according to Suffling. It is derived from *hey*, a form of *high*, which is from Old English *héah*.

I hope that Norfolk people still call the holly tree the *hulver*. Lydgate had this word as *hulfere* back in 1430. It is from the Old Norse *hulfr*, Ilex aquifolium to the botanists, holly to the rest of us. *Helve*, the handle of an implement, is ancient too. It survives in Scotland as well as in East Anglia, especially in the phrase 'to fling the helve after the hatchet', which means to throw good money after bad. Of Teutonic origin, it first appeared in English literature in 897, as *hielfe*, in a tract of King Aelfred's.

I am sure my Norfolk friends, Neila and Peter Drake, know these good words. I'll hain a glass with them soon. That's a promise.

JULY 2000

YOU'LL REMEMBER the deflated husband saying to his wife, as he looked out at the snow falling faintly through the universe in James Joyce's 'The Dead', 'I suppose you were in love with this Michael Furey, Gretta?' She answered, 'I was great with him at that time.' Well, I've had a note from a Japanese scholar about that phrase, *great with*, very friendly with. He asks about its origin, questioning my own theory that it is probably a direct translation of the Modern Irish phrase *mór le*.

Yes, I must confess that in acceding to the translation theory, the generally accepted one, I may have been remiss. Although Joyce himself seems to have thought of it as a translation, I should have pointed out that the Irish phrase is not, as far as I know, in either Old or Classical Irish. On the other hand, great and great with have been found in England since the 15th century, when an anonymous tract gave us, 'They are grete or homely to gydre.' 'The Duchess of York and the Duke of York are mighty great with her,' wrote Pepys in his diary for January 1668.

> My lord and he have grown so great,
> Always together, tête à tête

muses Swift half a century later. It was Swift's couplet that led my Japanese friend to question the translation theory.

Yes, great and great with are still common currency in many

places in rural England today. The *English Dialect Dictionary* gives a long paragraph on this particular use of *great*, found from Yorkshire to west Somerset, from where a correspondent wrote that 'grait [sic] is used only in the case of close friendship'. This is precisely what irked poor old Gabriel in 'The Dead'. So we must ask, did a direct translation of the Modern Irish phrase I mentioned give England great? The more I think of the matter, the more I doubt it. I have a feeling that the traffic went the other way.

I once heard an American scholar say that the phrase *a soft day*, an Irish euphemism for a persistently rainy day, shows 'the Irish genius for language'. He was struck by a line in a poem which went, 'A soft day, thank God,/A wind from the south with a honeyed mouth.' The *soft day*, he said, was direct from the Irish *lá* (day) *bog* (soft), as Irish as a banshee's bum, as they say around these parts.

The trouble is that Langland has *soft sonenday* in *Piers Plowman* back in 1362; almost a century earlier an anonymous writer has: 'This weder is softe, And this king hard.' The *EDD* has, from Warwickshire, 'The weather is falling to soft again', and from Durham, 'The common salutation on a rainy day is, "Soft!"'

Conclusion? Here we have a simple concept running parallel in two unrelated languages.

To my postbag. The word *crone*, a derogatory word for a wizened old woman, puzzles J.S. Long of Kidderminster. He (or is it she?) asks if it is related to *croon*, a lament, associated with the old women who sang them in days gone by at wakes and funerals in Scotland – and in Ireland too, I might add. 'Passing the house I heard a croon as if it were of a laden soul,' sang the Ayrshireman, Galt, in 1821.

No. Croon is from the Middle Dutch *kronen*, a lament; it's in the form *krónén* in Old High German. There seems to be no Old English cognate, strangely enough. The Irish *crónán* is related. Pronounced *crownaun*, the *-án* bit is simply a diminutive suffix; it was described by Jonah Barrington in his engaging *Personal Sketches*

(1820): 'The crownaun had no words. It was executed by drawing in the greatest portion of breath, and then making a sound like a humming-top.'

Crone, a hag, probably came into English directly from Norman French *carogne*, a carcass. It took on the meaning an ugly old woman in Middle English; Chaucer has 'This cursed crone' in 'The Man of Law's Tale'. The ultimate origin of carogne, and crone, is disputed, and it is thought by some to be some unattested Teutonic word that gave the word *kronje*, an old ewe, to Early Dutch. And if you don't fancy that explanation, try the Latin *caro*, flesh.

AUGUST 2000

DOWN THROUGH the years I have collected quite a few hilarious books, pamphlets and even copies of archive manuscripts dealing with the teaching of languages. One such manuscript was written by a hedge schoolmaster, that is a teacher who risked limb if not life in 18th-century Ireland at a time when education was denied by statute law to Roman Catholics. This teacher, poet and infamous toper, Muiris O'Gorman, left us his exposition of the Irish verb in all its tenses; it was based on a single word, *ól*, to drink; the result is very comical indeed. I also have a copy of a booklet by Canon O'Leary, a novelist and grammarian of the late 19th century. This particular booklet gained fame of a kind when the organizers of a Gaelic festival in Brooklyn placed an advertisement in a local newspaper, stating that the prizes in the fiddle-playing competition would be as follows: 'First prize, the invaluable treatise on the verbs *Is* and *Tá* [parts of the verb 'to be'] by Canon Peter O'Leary, inscribed by the author. Second prize, a case of Irish whiskey.' I am absolutely serious.

Last year I added to my collection by purchasing in the crypt of St-Martin-in-the-Fields, for less than a fiver, a little book called *English As She Is Spoke*, a modern edition of Senhor Pedro Carolino's

New Guide of the Conversation in Portuguese and English, first published in 1883. Pedro saw a market for a textbook that would initiate Portuguese and Brazilian students into the mysteries of English, and promptly wrote one. From the preface we see straight away that Pedro had about as much English as I have Malagasy: he seems to have relied on a Portuguese-French phrase book and a French-English dictionary. He ventured forth full of confidence into a linguistic minefield, and he was pleased with his work: 'We expect then, who the little book (for the care what we wrote him, and for her typographical correction) that may be worth the acceptation of the studious persons, and especialy of the Youth, at which we dedicate him particularly.'

Pedro first gives his young students some useful words under various headings. Under 'Of the Man' we find *the superior lip* and *the inferior lip*; also *the reins*. *The paint or disguise* and *the skate* are given under 'Woman Objects'. *The jack* and *the spark* are found under 'Kitchen Utensils'. Then comes 'Familiar Phrases'. Some examples:

> He do the devil at four.
> He burns one's self the brains.
> He was fighted in duel.
> They fight one's selfs together.
> He do want to fall.

James Millington's very amusing introduction to Senhor Pedro's little book examined these, but figure them out for yourselves; it's good fun searching for their Gallic origin.

Next comes a section on 'Familiar Dialogues'. Here we find 'The Fishing':

> That pond it sems me many multiplied of fishes.
> Let us amuse rather to the fishing.
> I do like-it too much.
> Here, there is a wand and some hooks.
> Silence! There is a superb perch! Give me quick the rod. Ah! there it is, it is a lamprey.

You mistake you, it is a frog! Dip again it in the water.

A hint as to Old Pedro's method of teaching a language he doesn't know is found under 'The french Language':

> Do you study?
> Yes, sir, I attempts to translate of french by portuguese.
> Do you know already the principal grammars rules?
> I am appleed my self at to learn by heart.
> Do you speak french alwais?
> Some times; though I flay it yet.
> You jest, you does express you self very well.

There is more. Our author has no qualms about translating letters by Racine and Montesquieu, flaying English to death in the process. He ends by giving us a section on what he calls 'Idiotisms and Proverbs'. Consider the following beauties:

> The necessity don't know the low.
> Of the hand to mouth, one lose often the soup.
> So much go the jar to spring that at last it break there.
> To build castles in Espagnish.
> The stone as roll, not heap up not foam.

Here French *mousse*, both foam and moss, banjaxed poor Pedro.

This little book is of delight from the *commencement* to the *fin*. It will your old heart lever.

SEPTEMBER 2000

I AM CURRENTLY engaged in compiling a dictionary of words that have entered the English of Ireland from languages other than Irish: Norse, Latin, Scots, Flemish, Dutch, German and, of course, the dialects of England. Now and again I come across words that the English dialect dictionaries have not recorded outside Ireland: I give them here in the hope that they live quietly in corners of England that the great Wright and his legion of workers on the *English Dialect Dictionary*, finished in 1906, have not recorded. I should be glad to hear from readers who have heard these words used as we use them on this side of the Irish Sea.

My Wexford granny used *convenient* when she meant near, close to. 'He lived convenient to me when I was young, I'm sorry to say,' she said of a politician she despised. Recently I heard some oldies from the border counties use the word; I got the feeling that convenient was 'genteel' speech. It is commonly used by auctioneers: 'Olde worlde cottage [i.e. a tumbledown shack], convenient to all amenities [i.e. a church, a graveyard and a pub].' I've also heard: 'It was convenient to morning when I got home.' As I say, the *EDD* could find no trace of this usage in England. It is ultimately from the Latin *conveniens*, present participle of *convenire*, to come together, to meet, unite, etc. There was also a French *convenient* recorded in the 15th century. I am tempted to speculate that our Irish convenient was an invention of the 18th-century hedge-schools, illegal Catholic schools that specialized in the classics and mathematics, and that gave a grounding to such illustrious men as Daniel O'Connell, Edmund Burke and Oliver Goldsmith. The hedge schoolmasters often knew more Latin than English and were famous inventors of words.

Another troublesome word is *collywest*. I have heard this in the south-east of Ireland. It may mean both nonsensical talk and astray. The learned journal, *Notes and Queries*, recorded 'Don't be talking collywest' in the west of Ireland in 1880. The Wexford folklorist and novelist Patrick Kennedy has, 'Oh, that's all collywest, says I,' in *The Banks of the Boro*, published in 1867. Recently, when I was lost in the south-eastern Blackstairs Mountains in a fog, a passing farmer told me that I should go *arsewards* (back) because I was as collywest as I could be.

An English friend tells me that there's a Collyweston in Northamptonshire. Did this place give us our collywest, and if so, how?

Latitat is in the *EDD* with the meaning, 'A noise, scolding; idle talk, chatter.' It had been recorded in Shropshire and Somerset. In Ireland we have retained the original meaning, more or less. And I'm anxious to know if it has survived across the water. I heard a Wicklow farmer complaining of trespass by his neighbour's cattle. 'I'm afraid I'll have to send him a latitat,' he said. This can mean either a letter from a solicitor or an ordinary missive complaining about the nuisance. Latitat has also taken on the meaning of a shot across the bows. 'He had been niggling me since the first scrum,' said a well-known rugby international to me recently, 'so I gave him one in the gob as a little latitat, like.'

Latitat is Latin, the third-person singular, indicative present of *latitare*, being in hiding, on the run: 'a writ which supposed the defendant to lie concealed and which summoned him to answer in the King's Bench', according to *Oxford*. It was first seen in print in Cooper's legal glossary of 1565: 'Annotare reos absentes, when a judge ordeineth persons accused in their absence to be sought for … as to send out as latitat.' Any sign of our Irish latitats in the England of 2000?

Finally, a word sent to me from Co. Waterford, in the south-east. 'Will ye look at the *gite* of her,' said an ancient lady on seeing a picture of a near-naked model in a Sunday newspaper supplement. This is a wonderful survival. Used for centuries in England in the sense of dress, I wonder does it survive in the speech of southern England? Chaucer has, 'She cam after in a gyte of reed' in 'The Reeve's Tale'; Gascoigne, in *Philomena* (1576), refers to 'A stately nymph Whose glittering gite so glinsed mine eyes.' The Old French has *guite*, a hat.

OCTOBER 2000

A FRIEND OF MINE who lives in Norwich paid me a visit recently. She and I went for a drink and during the course of the evening she, being all excira, as they pronounce 'excited' in Dublin, at seeing me after about forty years, spilled her gin and tonic over me. She asked the barman to get her a *dwile*, a word new to him, and to me. 'A cloth,' she explained, 'something to mop up this mess he's made.'

It seems that this word is confined to Suffolk and Norfolk; so the *English Dialect Dictionary* says. It is from the Dutch *dweil*, a mop, from the verb *dweilen*, to mop. It is probably a sailors' word, though by 1823, as Moor's glossary of Suffolk words shows, it had entered the farmhouse kitchen, with the meaning dish-cloth, towel. The Germans have *zwehle* for a towel; some common Teutonic ancestor hides in the distant past.

David Mitchell wrote to me from Horncastle, Lincolnshire, about a word he heard in that part of England recently, where to do a *slape* job means to make a mess of it through carelessness or indifference. A man he spoke to remarked that the council litter men once did a good job but over the years they had become slape. *Oxford* is of no help, he says.

It seems that the primary dialect meaning of this good and very old word is slippery; deceitful, untrustworthy, careless and indifferent seem to be figurative meanings. Lorne's book on Queen Victoria has this:

> The Princess [Victoria] was running about one wet morning on the terrace, when the gardener warned her to be careful, as the ground was 'slape'. She turned and asked: 'What is slape?' At that moment her heels flew up and she sat down suddenly on the slippery ground. 'That is slape, miss,' replied the old servant.

Slape in the Lincolnshire sense is also found in Yorkshire, where one of the glossaries recorded: 'A crafty, shuffling, unreliable person is said to be slape.' A Yorkshire *slapetail* is a cheat, an unsatisfactory workman. As I said, the word is old. It is recorded in the Towneley Mysteries about 1460: 'Who so will do after me Full slape of thrift then shall he be'; but the word must have been in use in England long before that, as it is certainly from Old Norse *sleipr*, slippery. Icelandic has *sleipur* and Norwegian *sleip*.

From Penrith in Cornwall came a letter from Rita Murray enquiring about the verb to shrim. She recently heard a neighbour complaining about clothes that had got 'shrimmed up in the washing machine'. *To shrim*, meaning to shrink, shrivel, also to shiver with cold and fright, seems to be confined nowadays to Cornwall and Devon, where it is also found as *shrimp*. I have also found shrim in a Gloucestershire glossary of the 19th century, defined as 'to shiver, or shrivel up with cold or fright; also of shrinkage in cooking'.

Scrim is very old, and for that reason alone I'm glad that it survives. It's from Old English *scrimman*, found only once in literature, in the *Leechdoms* of *c.* 1000, where there is a reference to 'scrimme & scrimme'.

Alan Morgan of Worthing, West Sussex and Roy Prince from York wrote about two different bobs. Mr Morgan tells me that his father, Reg, a Londoner and the composer of the popular songs 'Count Your Blessings' and 'Down Forget-me-not Lane', often used the expression, 'Well, swap me bob!' as an exclamation of surprise.

This expression can be traced to 19th-century London. It was used *sotto voce* by girls whenever they saw a likely lad pass by. The journal *Folk-Lore* says that the *bob* in question was a nosegay, a posy. Such exclamations of delight, surprise or interest are very hard to explain. Perhaps the girls of London were suggesting that they would swap their posies for a bit of a fling with his lordship. I'm guessing. This bob is of unknown origin. *Oxford* says that the Irish *baban*, a cluster, has been compared.

Mr Prince's *bob* is a verb that means to cheat or deceive. Nathan Bailey has the verb in his 1721 dictionary. Shakespeare, in *Troilus and*

Cressida, has: 'You shall not bob us out of our melody.' This is from Middle English *bobben*, itself from Old French *bober*, to mock, deceive.

NOVEMBER 2000

Not long ago, in a comfortable croft in the shadow of a Donegal mountain, I heard a young one, far too young at fifteen to be roaming in the gloaming with a fellow twice her age, explain to her mother that there was no harm in a bit of a dacker. I held my breath while the mother explained to me that a *dacker* was a stroll.

This particular dacker is known in Scotland, and in England's North Country, Yorkshire and Lincolnshire. What worried me was that where I come from, in south-eastern Ireland, a *dacker* is what vulgar people might call a quickie.

In my search for the origin of this word, I have found that in west Yorkshire *to dacker* means to work overtime, and to spin out work for the purpose of making overtime. In Scotland, and also in parts of the English Midlands, the verb dacker means to go about in a feeble state; to deteriorate, to get a relapse; to stagger, to totter; also to wave to and fro, as trees do in a winter wind. 'The fire dackers' has been recorded in Lincolnshire.

It was soon clear to me that these were different dackers; others sprouted up all over the place like mushrooms after rain. *To dacker* means 'to sprinkle' in Lincolnshire. 'Dacker the croak' is, or used to be, a Lincolnshire farmer's way of saying 'sprinkle water on the stack'. By the way, *croak* is from the Gaelic *cruach*; how the blazes did the word reach Lincolnshire? Anyway, another dialect dictionary told me that *to dacker* meant 'to engage in business in a piddling sort of way' in Scotland's Lothian; in the Western Isles *to dacker* means to lay out a dead body. On the eastern coast of Scotland the word crops up again, but in Aberdeen it means to search for stolen goods; also to challenge, to provoke a row. In Northumberland and in Lancashire we find the word as an adjective, used of the weather. It means unsettled. In Staffordshire I found that a *dacker person* is one whose sight is not good.

I have no idea, I'm afraid, where any of those dackers come from, with the exception of the one that means to go about in a feeble state, to stagger, to bend in the wind. This is from the Dutch *daeckeren*, to waver to and fro, from Middle Dutch *dakeren*. As to the rest, can anybody tell me anything about their origin? All the dialect dictionaries I've searched, even Wright's, have failed me.

To my postbag. *To frain* is a verb Martin Hunter of Barnsley heard in his youth in Yorkshire. It means to ask, enquire after. It is an old word; Langland has it in *Piers Plowman*: 'Ich ... frainede ful ofte of folk that ich mette ...' The word, I'm told, is still in use in Scotland and in Lancashire. It's from the Old English *fregnan*, to enquire. Old Norse has *fregna*.

Joyce Cooper is a friend of a friend of mine from Gloucester. She informs me that her friend still has a gleed for me. 'I bet you have no idea what that means,' she says. It means that your friend is pulling your leg, Joyce; but I do know that *gleed* means an ember, a flame, a glow, and that the word is still in use, according to the latest surveys, in Scotland, northern Ireland, Warwickshire, Leicestershire, Shropshire and in the North Country. Burns has, 'Cheery blinks the ingle gleed' in *Lady Onlie*. That dreadful Irish writer, Jane Barlow (*fl.* 1890) has 'A will o' the wisp luring him over the bog with its goblin glede' in her *Irish Idylls*. The word is from Middle English *glede*, burning coal, from Old English *gléde*, fire, flame.

A 21-gun salute to a lovely lady for whom I have a bit of an aul' gleed myself, Joanna Lumley, for solving a problem that has been bothering lexicographers for years: the origin of the word *fad*, an intense but short-lived fashion or craze; a personal idiosyncrasy or whim. 'Of uncertain origin', say the great dictionaries. From Malagasy, the official language of Madagascar, where fad has exactly the same meaning as the English word, says Miss Lumley. Malagasy belongs to the Malayo-Polynesian family; I once heard the late Anthony Burgess holding forth on the reluctance of lexicographers to search among this family of languages for the origin of many words designated 'origin unknown'.

DECEMBER 2000

As FAR AS I KNOW, the word *cantrip*, noun, verb and adjective, has never travelled further south than Northumberland and Cumbria. It is also found in both the highlands and the lowlands of Scotland. It has graced many's the fictional account of Christmasses past. As a noun it means a magic spell or incantation, a charm, a witch's trick, and as such Burns has it in *Tam O'Shanter*, where he writes of 'some devilish cantrip slight'.

Cantrip can mean an ordinary piece of mischief, as well; so Jean Baird of Aberdeen tells me. She was pleased, being a lover of words, to find that a note sent from her grandson's school, on the occasion of his being, once more, caught acting the maggot, referred to his cantrips. The verb means to perform very naughty, witch-like deeds. One of my dialect dictionaries quotes a poet called Whitehead who wrote of a lassie who 'oft went rompen wi' the deel To some kirkyard when't wind blew hard To cantrip o'er the deed.' Burns also used *cantrip* as an adjective, meaning evil, connected with the powers of darkness. In his 'Address to the Deil', appropriately enough, he speaks of a 'cantrip wit'.

Ivor Brown, who edited the *Observer* during the Second World War, mused about drinking words that come to mind at Christmas time. He found a solid splendour in the word *inebriation*: the inebriate, in contrast to the plastered, pissed, disguised or fluthered, stands, he claimed, like a gentleman with vine-leaves in his hair: 'He has the dignified tread of one who knows that he must, despite all causes and inclinations to sway, put up a seemly show of unwavering progress.' I am reminded of inebriated by a news item in a Dublin evening paper a few Christmasses ago, which told of a man who admitted to the judge, on the morning after the night before, that he had been a little inebriated all right, having sponged thirty-two pints in the course of the evening. 'That's four gallons!' computed the beak. 'The likes of you, with your fine job, can sponge it be the gallon,' replied the inebriate, 'but a poor oul' ballocks like me has to drink it be the pint.' Laughter in court. Probation Act applied; the spirit of Christmas prevailed.

Sponged, the man said. He didn't mean that he cadged his pints; he simply soaked them up. This is an old usage. Portia, you'll remember, was referring to drink when she refused to be married to a *spunge*, as Shakespeare spelled it. Lady Macbeth meant inebriated when she described the king's chamberlains as *spungy*:

> When in swinish sleep
> Their drenched natures lie as in a death,
> What cannot you and I perform upon
> His spungy officers.

William Cowper is remembered for his 'cups That cheer but not inebriate'; few remember that he was borrowing from George Berkeley, the Irish philosopher, who had already described tar-water as being 'of a nature so mild and benign and proportioned to the human constitution as to warm without heating, to cheer but not inebriate'. George's tar-water didn't quite catch on.

Maltworm is another word you'll hear in Dublin for a toper. It's not as common as it used to be, I'd say; there's an air of dark, smoke-filled snugs about it. It's old, though. There's a song in a collection of John Skelton's poems (*c.* 1550) that has:

> Then doth she troule
> To me the bolle
> As a goode malte-worme sholde.

And of course, Shakespeare has it in the first part of *Henry IV*, when Gadshill speaks of 'mustachio-purple-hued maltwormes'.

Toper is a word of uncertain origin. It is from the verb *tope*, to drink a lot. It's not very old; it made its appearance in literature in the 17th century. Dryden has, in his *Maiden Queen*: 'I'll tope with you, I'll sing to you, I'll dance with you.'

My favourite toper is not the inebriate with vine-leaves in his hair, or the lonely maltworm in his snug, or the legless sponge, but the chap who stands at the counter, ready to tell you what you want to hear, lifting your spirits should they need lifting, through a long, smoke-filled night. Cockneys have an inspired and endearing, if slightly vulgar, word for this philosopher of the saloon bar: he is a *piss-artist*.

A happy Christmas to you all.

JANUARY 2001

I FINISHED THE OLD YEAR in this column holding forth on words connected with various stages of intoxication, so I may as well start the new year with a word connected with the same subject that I heard during a visit to Norwich last October. A friend of mine told me of a device they had in Newcastle-upon-Tyne in the time of the Commonwealth and afterwards to help us combat the evils of gin, whisky and the Devil's buttermilk – Rev. Ian Paisley's delicious phrase for porter. Not for the puritan burghers of Newcastle to get the Protector-fearing clergy to chasten the people with fiery sermons; instead they invented a thing called the *drunkard's cloak*. By all accounts it put fear into even the most moderate of maltworms; you see, it was used by puritan women to put manners on their men. Indeed, it was invented by the mayor's wife.

My friend sent me an account culled from a tract called *England's Grievance Discovered in Relation to the Coal Trade*, published in 1655. It said:

> John Willis of Ipswich upon his oath said that he was in Newcastle six months ago. He further affirms that he hath seen men driven up and down the streets, with a great tub or barrel, opened in the sides, with a hole in one end, to put through their heads, and so cover their shoulders and bodies, down to the small of their legs, and then close the same, called the new-fashioned drunkard's cloak, and so make them march to the view of all beholders; and this is the punishment for drunkards and the like.

Another word comes up time after time in the old religious tracts of northern England, often in relation to those dangerous festivals at which drink was consumed in large quantities. It was frequently used of beer and ale. The word is *druvy*, and it meant turbid, not clear or transparent like water, the Lord's only drink, we are informed by some of the tracts, even at that bit of craic at Cana.

I'm told that the word is still in use in Cumbria and Northumberland, and that people use it of roads on which the snow has been made dirty by traffic.

Druvy is an old word. It's in Old and Middle English as *dróf*, turbid, troubled. Chaucer had *drovy*. 'He is lyk to an hors that seketh rather to drinken drovy or troubled water of the clere welle.'

I do wonder, though, if too much druvy ale could be responsible for the condition known as fey, mentioned so often in northern literature. *Fey* was an adjective, and the *Cornhill Magazine* of February 1880 tells us that the word was used of 'healthy people whose eyes displayed an unusual brightness, and who appear to act and speak in a wild and mysterious manner ... these were frequently said to be *fey*; that is doomed shortly to meet their death'. Could these not have been having a few quick ones on the sly?

The dialect dictionaries of yesteryear took this fey business very seriously. In Scotland, for instance, one source solemnly assures us that if the soap did not rise from the clothes a woman was washing, it was a sure sign that there was a fey person's clothes among them. And in the brewing of the ale for the New Year, if the wort boiled up in the middle of the pot, there was a fey person's drink in the pot.

The word is of Common Teutonic stock. There is the Old English *faege*, fated to die, near death, found in *Beowulf*, and the Old High German *feigi*, with the same meaning. Burns has the word, in *Sheriffmuir*:

> Thro' they dashed, and hew'd, and smash'd
> Till fey men died awa, man.

Well, swap me bob, but I seem to have made an hors's ars of things, as old Chaucer might have written, when I wrote about that London expression recently. I have had a spate of letters on the subject, all telling me that *swap me bob* is merely a euphemistic way of saying, 'So help me, God.' Thanks to my correspondents. I hope Alan Morgan of Worthing, West Sussex, will forgive me.

A happy New Year to you. *Fan óg*, (fonogue) as we say, stay young, until the days begin to lengthen again this time next year.

FEBRUARY 2001

I HOPE Alice Thomas Ellis won't mind me writing about God, or at least about words and phrases associated with him. It is hard to believe, but nevertheless true, that not so long ago The Man Above, as he is known in Ireland, was so revered that even disguising forms of his name, used as quasi-oaths or exclamations of surprise, were frowned upon. I remember my grandmother wincing when a neighbour's child said 'by goxty', a mild expletive used by Yeats in his *Folk Tales* in 1888. The dialect dictionaries have similar little oaths, if they can be called such, from many parts of England: *by gox* was recorded in Northumberland, *by gock* in Durham, *gocks* in Cumbria; while common exclamations of wonder and satisfaction took the form of compounds such as *gocks bobs, gocks dillies, gock son, gock wuns, gock wunters, goke a day* all over the North Country.

God was very much part of country life in the old days. In Yorkshire *God's biddings* were the Ten Commandments. *God cake* was a cake sent by godparents to their godchildren on New Year's Day. *Notes and Queries*, that marvellous learned journal, still going strong, has this from the Coventry of 1856:

> God cakes are used by all classes, and vary in price from a halfpenny to one pound. They are invariably made in a triangular shape, an inch thick, and filled with mincemeat. So general is the use of them that the cheaper sorts are hawked about the streets.

In the Irish language mentally ill people were known as 'daoine le Dia', which translates as *God's people*; in Sussex they were known as *God's children*. In Thomas Hardy country a *god-forgive-me* was a jug used for warming ale. He has, 'Jacob stooped to the god-forgive-me, which was a two-handled tall mug standing in the ashes, cracked and charred with heat,' in *Far From the Madding Crowd*. *God's good* or *Gosgood* were Kentish for yeast and barm. A tract of 1736 explains:

> When the success of anything was precarious, the good wives

were used to bless or exorcise it. So at this day after having beat the barm into the ale, when it is in the fat they always Cross it with two long strokes with the hand from side to side.

God's good, therefore, I would suppose to be a form of blessing or exorcising, or at least the two first words of such a form.

The southern Irish, the Shetland Islanders and the people of the Kentish coast called a shipwreck a *Godsend*, blasphemously, many of the old dictionaries said. In England's North Country, and in my own Wexford, a *godspeed* is a wooden partition behind the front door of a farmhouse to keep out the wind. So called, it is thought, because leave-takings or good-byes were said there.

God appears too in the names of many plants. *God's eye* is the germander speedwell, *Veronica chamaedrys*, in Lincolnshire and in Devon; *God's grace* the field wood-rush, *Luzula campestris*, in Cheshire; the young leaves of the hawthorn are called *God's meat* in Warwickshire.

In the case of birds and animals, God was not forgotten. The robin is *God's bird* in Ireland and Warwickshire. This is because a drop of blood fell on the little bird's breast from the Cross, staining it forever, according to the folklore. The ladybird is known in Cornwall, Hampshire and in Ireland as *God's cow* or *God's colly cow*; in parts of Lancashire as *God's horse*. Kill the little thing at your peril. In Hampshire the children had a rhyme: 'God a'mighty's colly cow, Fly up to Heaven, Carry up ten pound, And bring down eleven.' In Warwickshire the swallow was known as *God's scholar*. In Somerset, *God Almighty's bread and cheese* is the wood-sorrel, *Oxalis acetosella*.

God help me and *God help us* are exclamations claiming pity, used after the names of certain places. *Mayo, God help us!* is used in Ireland to insult people from that western county at football matches. *Notes and Queries* of 1850 tells me that Melverly, in Shropshire, once went by the soubriquet *Melverly God Help* because it was frequently inundated in winter.

Well, now that I've given God his due, may I be so bold as to ask him to keep you, or as they say hereabouts, to look to you.

MARCH 2001

I ENVY A SON of mine who is building a house in Co. Waterford, in the south of this sainted isle I live in. Before him lies a lush valley. To his left there is the range of the lovely Comeragh mountains; to his right, the Atlantic. As I was discussing his plans with an architect friend the other night, the word fornication cropped up. I raised a quizzical eyebrow, as Mr Wooster might say. *Fornication*: an arching, a vaulting, he explained. This is adapted from the Latin, *fornicatio*, from *fornicatus*, vaulted, from *fornix*, a vault. Is it, you may ask, related to the word for how's-your-father, or *houghmagandie*, as they say in Scotland and in Ulster: voluntary sex between a man (in restricted use, an unmarried man) and an unmarried woman? It is indeed, for this tally-ho, to use another Irish euphemism for it, is from Old French *fornication*, ultimately from *fornix*, a brothel; originally an arch, or vault, a feature of the old Roman wattling shops (wattle, a stick, geddit?).

But there is another *fornicate* to be found in the old glossaries from Cheshire, Warwickshire and Shropshire. It means to fabricate, invent falsehoods; to tell lies. 'It wuz a downright lie, an' 'e can fornicate 'em as fast as a 'orse can trot.' Hence *fornicating*, participle adjective, false, treacherous, deceitful, and *fornicator*, one who invents or tells lies. From Shakespeare's country Wright has, 'Don't you 'a' nuthin' to do wi' Charlie Styles, 'e's a fornicatin' 'ound.' And if that's not enough, from Sussex *to fornicate* means to dawdle, to waste time.

The Scots have *horbgorble* for what the Americans call fooling around, fumbling or, as we say, mooching. No fornication here, but behaviour that oldies of yesteryear believed to be a stepping-stone to houghmagandie and Hell. To the late Ivor Brown I owe horbgorble, a word that has reached the shores of America. A correspondent of Brown's recollected the trial of a young Caithness man for alleged assault on a servant girl. The case was brought not by the girl but by her employer, a puritanical gentleman who was, he felt, acting *in loco parentis*, even though the lass was over the age of consent. The magistrates wanted to hear her side of the story, and she explained that her boyfriend was only horbgorblin' when her employer caught them at it. Her explanation was readily understood by the court; the employer was considered to be a meddling old fool and the case was dismissed. I have no idea where horbgorble comes from.

But what about the wonderful Scots and Ulster *houghmagandie*? This marvellous fanciful formation for full-blooded fornication may be from the Scots noun *hough*, the back part of the thigh, plus the adjective *canty*, brisk, lively. Burns wrote of the *Holy Fair*:

> There's some are fou [full] o' love divine
> And some are fou o' brandy,
> And monie jobs that day begin
> May end in houghmagandie...

Nabokov used the great Scots word in *Pale Fire*. 'She would have preferred him to have gone through a bit of wholesome houghmagandie with the wench.'

No doubt a lot of horbgorblin', not to mention houghmagandie, takes place on summer evenings in the scugs of England's North Country. June Rigney, who lives in north Yorkshire, wrote to me about *scug*, which means shelter. The word is also found in Scotland in various forms, *skig*, *scoog* and *skough* among them. The Shetland islanders have *skjug*.

Originally the word meant a shadow; then it came to mean shelter afforded by a rock, bush or the like. Its origin is Old Norse *skugge*, shadow. Old English has *scuwa*, shade. Norwegian has *skugge*, shade, and, in dialect, darkness and fog; Danish has *skygge*.

The word is in Scots literature since 1513, when Dunbar wrote of Jupiter hiding the heavens with scug. There is a verb *scug* as well. It means to protect, shelter. In an Edinburgh court in 1950 a young man arrested while lying on top of a young lady in a park solemnly told a court that he was only scuggin' her. It had started to rain, you see. The beak let him off with a caution after he explained the verb to him.

My son informs me that in Cornwall, where he lives, a *scug* is both a squirrel and a pretty young woman. The origin of this scug is unknown.

APRIL 2001

I WAS DELIGHTED to hear from two *Oldie* readers that correspondence they have had with the *Oxford English Dictionary* has resulted in that great authority on the language agreeing to make changes: an unusual occurance, let me tell you.

Nick Flowers wrote to me from Chichester about his *Oxford* experience. I'll let him tell his own tale:

> When I was a film sound recordist working for the BBC Nationwide television programme in the early seventies, we shot a story in Gawsworth Hall in Cheshire about a character called Maggoty Johnson, who lived in the 18th century. Maggoty (so called either because his face was eaten up with smallpox or because he was a 'maggot', in the language of the times, a professional jester) entertained the quality at Gawsworth and the area around. But in 1729 he produced in London a farrage – he called it an opera – called *Hurlothrumbo*. It was very poor indeed. I know: I've read it. But the Duke of Montagu, for reasons best known to himself, but one suspects that he had in mind a vast practical joke to take a rise out of the gullible public, promoted the project, and it succeeded beyond Maggoty's wildest dreams. Maggoty eventually retired to

Gawsworth and died there, and that was the end of the film story.

About six months ago the memory of Maggoty came back to me, and I looked up *hurlothrumbo* in the *OED*. It wasn't there. I asked *Oxford* about this and their reply was that Hurlothrumbo was a proper name, the name of a play, and no more. I suspected that there was more to to this than met the eye, so I indulged in some pretty superficial research and turned up some interesting evidence. John Byrom, a Manchester poet and inventor of the term 'tweedledum and tweedledee', tells us in his diary that a phrase had entered the English language that suggests that if anything is inconsistent, it is 'mere hurlothrumbo as a noisy orator or preacher'. And as late as the 1930s *Roget* has the word meaning bugbear, or bogeyman.

The *OED* has accepted my findings and will have hurlothrumbo in the great dictionary as soon as is convenient. I can't tell you how good it feels to have made my mark, however insignificantly, upon the history of English language and to have Maggoty's word – if it *is* his – put in its proper place.

Well done, Mr Flowers!

Dympna Lonergan is a Dublin woman who lives now in Happy Valley, South Australia. She wrote to tell me of her disquiet at the *Oxford* discussion of the phrase 'the cockles of my heart', which was first seen in print in English in 1671. Seemingly not quite sure about the origin of the phrase the great dictionary suggests, tentatively, the Latin *corculum*, diminutive, of *cor*, heart. But it goes on to quote Robert Latham, a 19th-century authority on etymology: 'The most probable explanation lies (1) in the likeness of the heart to a cockleshell; the base of the former being compared to the hinge of the latter; (2) in the zoological name for the cockle being *Cardium*, from Greek *kardia*, heart.'

Fair enough, says Dympna. But what about the Irish *cochall*, which is pronounced as near as dammit 'cockle', and is used in the phrase *cochall mo chroí*, the cockles of my heart? *Cochall* is the Irish for the pericardium, the membranous sac enclosing the heart. The word has been in Irish for over a thousand years, its original meaning being a husk, shell, covering. It is from Latin *cucullus*, a covering for the head in wet weather.

What put doubts into Dympna's mind? I am much too modest to tell you. But the good news is that her speculation is being given credence by *Oxford*, and one day she will find herself ranked with Latham and company in the great authority's discussion of cockle.

MAY 2001

IT SADDENS ME sometimes to find so many good dialect words marked 'obsolete' in the dictionaries. I came across one such the other day: one I heard in 1970 from an old man who lived in south-east Wexford, in the Anglo-Norman Barony of Forth, where their own brand of Middle English survived as a complete linguistic entity until the middle of the 19th century. Old Phil Wall, then over ninety, showed me some pewter dishes he had on his dresser, and lamented the fact that once upon a time he had a complete garnish of them. Not a trace could I find of this *garnish* until, years afterwards, I found the word in a Yorkshire dictionary, marked 'obsolete', and with the gloss, 'A set of pewter dishes.'

The Wexford Barony of Forth was once famed for starving the merchants of nearby Wexford town. You see, the Forth people made all their own clothes; their coopers made all their furniture, including wooden platters, cups and saucers; they brewed their own beer, and they even made their own pewter. There is mention of the word garnish in Holinshead's *Chronicles* of 1580, in a gloss on the word found in the 1440 dictionary *Promptorium Parvulorum Sive Clericorum*: there is no doubt in my mind, given Holinshead's interest in the dialect of south-east Wexford, that the writer had Mr Wall's place in mind: 'In some places beyond the sea a garnish of good flat English pewter of an ordinarie making is esteemed almost so pretious as the like number of vessels that are made of fine silver.' Harrison's *Description of England* (1587) gives further information: 'Such furniture of househould of this mettall [pewter], as we commonlie call vessell, is sold vsuallie by the garnish, which doeth containe twelue platters, twelue dishes and twelue saucers.'

Does the word survive anywhere in England, I wonder? Garnish, by the way, is from Old French *garniss-*, lengthened stem of *garnir*, to provide, prepare. Compare the Modern French *garnir*, to furnish. The Medieval Latin *guarnire* lurks in the background: the source too, of Old Spanish *guarnir*, Modern Spanish *guarnecer* and the Italian *guarnire, guenire*.

Mrs Fiona Wade of Mollington, near Chester, wrote to me about a word of her father's, puckle. The good man was a Church of Scotland minister and his daughter is writing up his memoirs. He had organized a midnight service for the first time, and as he heard no sound from the church as he was preparing in the vestry he had the awful thought that nobody had turned up. But the Beadle assured him that there was 'a gey puckle' waiting: and sure enough, the church was full. What, Mrs Wade asks, is a puckle? She worries that a slip of the pen may have made *puckle* of *muckle*.

No. *Puckle* is a Scots variant of *pickle*, an infinite number; a few. Jamieson's *Scottish Dictionary* defines the word as a grain of corn, and gives the extended meanings, a single seed, any minute particle, a small quantity, a few. The word's origin is unknown. *Gey*, considerable, especially of quantity or amount, is a variant of *gay*, from Old French *gai*. The ulterior etymology is disputed, but *Oxford* says that the sense slack, not close-fitting, is recorded in all the Roman languages. Anyway, the Beadle's *gey puckle* means a considerable amount.

From the lovely, and alas, endangered puckle to the very much alive and vulgar phrase *pissed as a newt*. J.H. Bentley, writing from Aukland, New Zealand, tells me that when he read what I wrote here connecting the phrase *on the batter* with the building term *bat-*

ter, meaning to lean from the perpendicular, he wondered how the small-tailed amphibian could have become an index for drunkenness. Then, eureka!

> I write as a Mancunian [he says]. In the north-west of England, one could be 'pissed as a Newton'; elsewhere the phrase became corrupted to 'pissed as a newt'. The reference is to the oblique mirror on a Newtonian telescope. If you were staggering drunk, that is declining from the vertical, or oblique, you were pissed as a Newton.

I see.

Anthony Burgess once said to me that the nicest thing about this science of lexicography is the fun you can get out of it.

Thanks, Mr Bentley.

JUNE 2001

WHERE I LIVE the elder-tree, *Sambucus nigra*, is regarded as cursed. One should never bring a branch of it into the house; it is said that it is impossible to burn. Such considerations never stopped us when we were young from removing the pith from elder rods to make very effective peashooters. John Walpole from Durham tells me that in Cumberland, Wesmorland, Yorkshire and Lancashire, the elder-tree is known as the *bourtree*, sometimes *boretree* and *boortree*, and it seems to be regarded as unlucky in the north of England and in Scotland as well as in Ireland. A Donegal woman once told me that the bourtree was cursed because it was the tree Christ was nailed to. *Chambers' Popular Rhymes*, a fascinating anthology published in 1870, echoes this in a piece from southern Scotland: 'Bourtree, bourtree, crooked rung, Never straight and never strong, Ever bush and never tree, Since Our Lord was nailed to ye.' In parts of southern Ireland the bourtree is considered unlucky because the oldies thought that Judas hanged himself from it.

Mr Walpole's letter concerned the word's origin. I can't help, I'm afraid. Origin unknown, *Oxford* says, rightly discounting the plausible derivation from *to bore*, verb, suggested by John Ray's glossary of 1691, as being inconsistent with the earliest and the dialect form. Ray says that the boretree is named 'from the great pith in the younger branches which children commonly bore out to make potguns of them'. And as to the tree being named from *bower*, meaning arbour, that's most unlikely as regards meaning.

Mrs Jane Henry, who lives in Hexham, Northumberland, asks me about the word *crame*, noun, apparently confined to her native place and to Scotland. An interesting and much-travelled word this is. It means a merchant's booth or temporary shop, set up at fairs, races and the like; a stall in a market. From the noun we have the compounds *crame-stand*, a stand on which goods are displayed for sale in stalls; *crame-ware*, goods sold at stalls or booths, and *crame-wife*, a woman who sells goods from a stall at a fair. There is a verb *to crame*: to hawk goods by carrying them from place to place for sale. Hence the noun *cramer*, a pedlar, a hawker of goods.

Crame was adopted in 15th century Scotland from Middle Dutch (Flemish) or Middle Low German *kraeme*, which has survived in Modern Dutch as *kraem*, tent, booth, stalls. A 1477 Charter of James III of Scotland refers to 'The Cramys of chapmen'. In 1560 an Aberdeen Register tells of a poor man 'desyring support etc, to help him to ayn crayme, that he may trawell to win his lifting in the cuntray'. The original sense, which can be deduced from Old High German, was 'tent-covering, awning'. In the transferred sense, merchandise, wares, the word travelled to northern and eastern Europe with German traders and it probably came to Scotland in the same way. I'm glad it survives.

A letter from Peter Stone of Putney, London, about *to scug*, verb, to shelter, protect; also a noun meaning 'shadow', from the Old Norse *skugge*, shadow, shade. I wondered in the March column why Cornish oldies call both a squirrel and a pretty young woman a *scug*. Mr Stone points out that squirrel is from Latin *sciurus*, itself from two Greek words meaning 'shade' and 'tail', from the belief that squirrels used their tails as a sun-shade. *Scug*, a young woman, we can link to the poor little squirrel; a pretty tail seems to be of great importance in the male Cornish oldies' appraisement of female pulchritude.

My congee to Mr Stone. If you are from southern Scotland, from East Anglia, from Oxford or from Cornwall, the chances are you will know what that means. *Congee*, noun, is a bow, obeisance; you may also use it as a verb; Kate Anderson from Norwich wonders where it came from. 'I alighted from my horse and drew near to her with congees,' wrote Stevenson in *Catriona*. Kit Marlowe has this: 'And with a lowly congé to the ground, The proudest lords salute me.' Coles' dictionary of 1678 defines the French *congé* as 'corpus inclinare'. Vale.

JULY 2001

IN MY PART of the world, and perhaps in yours, dear reader, *higgledy-piggledy* means disorder; jumbled confusion. This nice rhyming compound may or may not be founded on 'pig'. The famous 1700 *Dictionary of the Canting Crew* was the first to suggest that it is; it has 'higgeldy piggeldy, all together as hoggs and piggs lie'. As far as I know, John Florio, Anne of Denmark's tutor in Italian, English and, it was rumoured, the carnalities, was the first to record the word in his wonderfully quirky dictionary of 1598, *The Worlde of Wordes*. He defines *alla rappa* as 'snatchingly, higgildie-piggeldie, shiftingly, nap-and-run', whatever the hell that means.

While I was looking for the origin of the compound for Mrs Rachel Blake of Sheffield, I found to my surprise that it means something else entirely in Cheshire: they have a phrase there, *Higgledy-piggledy Malpas shot*, which means serving all alike, making no difference between people. An old story connects it to James I; William III is the man in question in another folkloric version, which goes like this:

> Before his invasion of England William travelled to England incognito, with a view to certify himself of the state of the national feeling towards himself and his colleagues, and, coming to Malpas, betook himself to the inn for his dinner, a repast which he happened to share with the Rector and the Curate of the parish. The meal over, the Curate proposed to the Rector to divide the payment of the 'shot', that of the stranger included, between them. To this, the Rector, who enjoyed in the neighbourhood the reputation of being a miser, strenuously objected, exclaiming, 'Certainly not! Higgledy-piggledy all pay alike,' and so it was arranged. But when William was seated on the throne, the Rector of Malpas, among others, made a journey to London to worship the rising sun. The King no sooner saw him than he reminded him of the incident, and compelled him to resign a moiety of the parish to his Curate, also with the title of Rector, on the principle embodied in his own apothegm, 'Higgledy-piggledy, all pay alike.' And from that day forward there have been two Rectors of Malpas.

Shot, payment, contribution, is interesting. From Old English *scéotan*, shoot, it first appears in literature in an old song from about 1475: 'On[e] cast downe her schott and went her wey. Gossip, quod Elenore, what did she pay? Not but a peny.' Does the word still survive?

From Jeanne Marshall of King's Lynn in Norfolk comes a query about the word *kickshaw*. This was Jeanne's mother's word for a worthless thing, a knick-knack. This meaning is also found in Scotland, Northumberland, Cumbria and Devon. I see that in West

Yorkshire a *kickshaw* is a proud, vain person; and there is still another meaning to be found in Devon and Cornwall: an untidy dresser, a streel, as we say in Ireland. Wright's great *English Dialect Dictionary* has not, surprisingly, got the meaning I have heard in my native Wexford: a fancy dish, a dainty. Shakespeare has it in *Henry IV, part II*: 'a joynt of mutton and any pretty little tinie kickshawes'. His contemporary, Thomas Dekker, speakes of 'cowslip sallads and kickchoses', but my old friend Florio, mentioned above, shows us where the word originated. Under the headword *carabozzado* he wrote: 'a kinde of daintie dish or quelque chose vsed in Italie'. It seems that in the 17th century the commonest forms of the French followed the pronunciation *que' que chose*. This was regarded at the time as the height of elegance, and is still current in colloquial French. Gradually, kickshaw took over completely and by the 19th century even a snob like Thackery used it instead of the French: in a tribute to George Cruikshank he has: 'The chef is instructing a kitchen-maid how to construct some rascally French kickshaw.'

Chaucer preferred good old English *kichils* to foreign kickshaws. His word is still found in East Anglia. Kichils, or *kitchels*, are flat, sweet little Christmas cakes of a triangular shape. Thanks to Jeanne Marshall for this word, too.

AUGUST 2001

IN EVELYN WAUGH'S *Put Out More Flags*, which I have been rereading lately, I came on the sentence: 'This formidable man of his own age was another kettle of fish.' I have often wondered how a *kettle of fish* could have Waugh's meaning, and, as well as that, a muddle, a mess, an awkward state of things. Fielding in *Tom Jones* (1749) has, 'Fine doings at my house! A rare kettle of fish I have discovered at last.'

Kettle, the thing we boil water for tea in, is Common Teutonic. The Old English is *cetel*; a gloss from *c.* 700 has *cetil*; the Old Saxon is *ketel*; the Vikings cooked venison in a *ketill*. All these words were probably from the Latin *catillus*, diminutive of *catinus*, a food vessel. Fair enough; I suppose that the old Romans cooked fish in a *catillus* or *catinus*, but this fact didn't help me with Waugh's phrase or with the observation by a golf commentator recently that Mr Tiger Woods was, by reason of his overshooting the green and landing in a grove of trees, in a fine kettle of fish.

Folklore is often a help in tracing the origin of phrases. The *Berwick Journal* of 1896 tells us that our phrase means a fête champêtre at which salmon is the chief item:

> As far back as 1675, this special form of festivity was known on the classic Borderland, for the Guild of Berwick-upon-Tweed in this year made a treat of a kettle of salmon on the riverside. A Tweedside kettle is after the fashion of an up-river picnic, but it has its own peculiar characteristics. The company foregather under a great marquee pitched on the pleasantly situated green-sward at South Bells Fishery – on the English side of the Tweed, about four miles up from Old Berwick Town – and after doing full justice to the salmon, 'newdrawn frae the Tweed' by the net fishers who ply their avocation not a stone's throw away, a short toast is honoured.

Games followed, some of which reminded me of the games forbidden by the Irish clergy after Patterns, or saints' feast-day celebrations, in the 19th century. Sexy games, I'm afraid, or, as the Scots had it, houghmagandie.

Scott tells us in a note on our phrase in *St Ronan* (1824) that the cauldron in which the fish was cooked was 'thickened with salt to the consistence of brine', and that the fish were thrown into the boiling water while still alive. Do they still have their Kettle of Fish down-river from Berwick? At any rate, here, I take it, is the origin of our phrase; the meanings mess, muddle, etc. came from the primitive culinary method used on the banks of the Tweed in the old days.

I had to smile the other night when an American television commentator described President George Dubya as a natural. He was praising his ability to handle the questions of a nebby foreign press on issues such as global warming and Star Wars by giving evasive answers. In Scotland, Ireland, Cumberland, Yorkshire, Lancashire, Cheshire, Somerset, Devon and Cornwall, a *natural*, according to the *English Dialect Dictionary*, means an idiot; an imbecile, a half-witted person. Scott, in *The Bride of Lammermoor*, has, 'What picture, you natural! I used to think you only a scape-grace, but I believe you will turn out to be a born idiot.' Shakespeare knew this meaning of natural. In *Romeo and Juliet* he has, 'This drivelling love is like a great natural.' To Sir Thomas More is given the honour of being the first man of note to use natural in this way in literature. In 1553 he wrote to a friend: 'It could never be done more naturally, not though he that wrote it were even a very natural in dede.' As for me, and for my opinion of Dubya, may I quote Steele, who in 1722 wrote of a thorn in his side: 'I own the man is not a Natural, he had a very quick Sense, though very slow Understanding.'

By the way, *nebby*, used above, is Scots and Ulster English for impertinent. From Middle English *neb*, a bird's beak; hence humorously, the mouth; hence *nebby*, cheeky, saucy, one who uses the mouth too much. Your man from Warwickshire knew this usage: in *A Winter's Tale* he has: 'How she holds up the neb, the bill to him.'

SEPTEMBER 2001

OBSOLETE WORDS fascinate me. So many good ones have died, and in many cases we'll never know why. Ambrose Bierce remarked in his 1911 classic, *The Devil's Dictionary*:

> Obsolete, *adj*. No longer used by the timid. Said chiefly of words. A word which some lexicographer has marked obsolete is ever thereafter an object of dread and loathing to the fool writer, but

if it is a good word and has no exact modern equivalent equally good, it is good enough for the good writer. Indeed a writer's attitude toward 'obsolete' words is as true a measure of his literary ability as anything except the character of his work.

Some good words died out due to changes in social life. The good North Country and Yorkshire word *garsom* is one of them. It meant an earnest penny, a fore-gift, or God's penny, to bind or confirm a new labourer on a farm. The Medieval Latin was *gersuma*, 'hoc est pecunia data in pactionem', according to Spelman's glossary. But the Latin word was a borrowing, I think. Old English has *gersom*, treasure, from 1090; the Old Norse had *gersemi*, a costly thing. Just beneath this old word in the dialect dictionaries you'll find *garston*, a Somerset word for an enclosed yard used for fattening cattle. Gone now, for whatever reason. It had been used since about 1000. The Old English was *gærstún*.

And why did so many of the *dis*-words disappear? *Disheighten*, verb, was used in Gloucestershire until recently. It meant to disparage, disgrace. *Disjune* is Scots. A noun, it meant breakfast. Scott, in *Old Mortality*, referred to 'that famous morning when his most sacred Majesty partook of his disjune at Tillietudlem'. This is from the Old French *desjun*. *Disknowledge*, verb, was used in Cornwall. It meant to be ignorant of, not to know; also to deny, disown. 'Q', otherwise Sir Arthur Quiller Couch, has, 'Sam suddenly found that he disknowledged the Spanish for "corpse",' in *Troy Town*. A Cornish glossary quotes a policeman in evidence: 'He did not disknowledge it, sir.' The north Yorkshire *dispart* has gone too. It meant to pull asunder, to separate. In one of his tracts Milton has: 'As often as any great schisme disparts the church.'

Dispeace meant a Scottish disagreement, dissention, disquiet. Gone. So too is the noun *disparage*, something Scottish mothers were wont to worry a lot about when casting about for eligible husbands for their daughters. It meant inequality of social rank, and more importantly, inequality of bank balances. From the Old French *desparage*, inequality of rank in marriage, itself from the

Medieval Latin *disparagium*, 'inequality in blood, honour, dignity', according to Skeat.

But enough of this moaning. Let me turn to a marvellous book I've been reading – the one from which I got the paragraph from *The Devil's Dictionary* quoted above. *Words on Words*, by David and Hilary Crystal, is an anthology of quotations about words, over 5000 of them in all, under sixty-four different headings. Here's Frank Zappa on rock journalists: 'People who can't write interviewing people who can't talk for people who can't read.' On bilingualism, Somerset Maugham: 'It is good to be on your guard against an Englishman who speaks French perfectly; he is very likely to be a cardsharper or an attaché in the diplomatic service.' A good answer to the old question, what's the difference between language and dialect? 'A language is a dialect that has an army and a navy,' answered Max Weinrich in his 1973 *History of the Yiddish Language*. On words as weapons, our authors quote Marcus Aurelius: 'A candour affected is a dagger concealed.' And here too is Phyllis McGinley:

> Sticks and stones are hard on bones
> Aimed with angry art,
> Words can sting like anything
> But silence breaks the heart.

A few random favourites from this delightful book. On women and words, Marcel Achard has this to say: 'Women like silent men. They think they're listening.' And lastly, something to encourage all harmless drudges like me. Boswell had told Johnson that he was collecting Scots words:

Johnson: By collecting those words you will do a useful thing towards the history of the language.
Boswell: But of what use will it be, sir?
Johnson: Never mind the use, do it.

OCTOBER 2001

LORNA MURRAY, a correspondent from Lancaster, has the good fortune to own a holiday cottage not very far from where Wordsworth could not but be gay among the daffodils. What troubles Lorna is the name of the cottage, *Birch How*.

The word how is not found on my side of the Irish Sea, as far as I know. The word is common wherever the Norsemen had an influence, from Orkney to England's North Country, East Anglia, Somerset and Devon. Scotland, like Ireland, does not have the word or any of its variants, *hogh*, *hoh*, *hoo*, *howack*, *howie*, *haugh*, *hough*, all found in English place-names. The *how* was a prehistoric tumulus, and it is now applied to hillocks whether artificial or natural. In places the Viking connection is remembered in folklore. Writing of Orkney in 1884, Fergusson, in his charming book, *Rambles*, said that 'it was a matter of common occurrence for the Norsemen to break open a howe in the expectation of finding treasure'. This was probably correct; in Ireland, to our shame, I admit it, farmers have been known to level these tumuli in the hope of finding treasure the Norse had buried.

The Vikings burying treasure? Oh yes. You see, the gold and silver they had fecked from the Irish monasteries was so heavy that they buried it in the *lios*, anglicized *liss*, the fairy mound, home of the leprechaun, intending to come back for it later. Of course the leprechauns put spells on the Vikings to ensure that they would get lost when they returned. You never heard that? Where do you think the leprechauns, who were only the fairies' shoemakers after all, get their crocks of gold?

I think we must give credit to Hampole for first using the word how in literature. In his translation of one of the Psalms, done in 1330 or thereabouts, he has, 'The shadow of it couyrd howis'; *howis* was glossed as *montes*. Vigfusson's magisterial dictionary of Old Icelandic, which *Oxford* has allowed to go out of print, tells me that the word is from Old Norse *haugr*, a mound.

Joan Marshall, who lives near Hillesley, Wotton-under-Edge,

Gloucester, has sent me a most interesting addendum to what I had to say about nice kettles of fish. She mentioned the dialect word *keddle*, a fish trap, and enclosed in her letter a sketch of one from Dorothy Hartley's *Food in England*. She quotes from the book:

> Fish traps of this kind were legally used in runs of fish, or to stop some mill race in private waters, but when they were set up at random in open rivers they could ruin the fishing of an entire district in one season.

It would seem, my correspondent writes, that the term 'a pretty keddle of fish' could mean either satisfaction at a mixed bag of fish, or exasperation at the disruption caused by setting one. This explains the term 'a nice kettle of fish' better than the *English Dialect Dictionary*'s ramblings about Berwick's kettle that I mentioned here. The *EDD*, by the way, doesn't have keddle, but then, it doesn't claim to have every dialect word in existence.

Should my friend George Dubya ever visit Northern Ireland and engage in his backslapping routine in one of the local pubs, he would be well advised not to shout, 'Howdy!' as a greeting, in case people thought his wife was in urgent need of the ministrations of a midwife. Margaret Forbes, who lives in Kilmarnock, Scotland, asked about *howdie*, which is really a Scots word. They also have the compound *howdie-wife* for midwife in Ulster; to be *howdying* means to be ready to give birth. Scott has the word *houdie* in *Guy Mannering*: 'The laird's servant ... rade express by this e'en to fetch the houdie.' The etymology of the word, which is what Mrs Forbes wrote about, is obscure, but the *EDD* says that it's an appellative (like brownie, etc.) from *hold*, Old English for friendly, gracious, kind. Maybe.

A word about *to kensill*, to thrash, beat severely, still used in the North Country, according to Douglas Grant of Barrow, in Cumbria, who asks about its origin. It comes from the Old Norse *kennsla*, teaching, would you believe. I'm sure many an oldie would!

NOVEMBER 2001

AN OLD TRAVELLING man of my acquaintance, too old now to break horses, was having a pint with me in our local. I asked him about the merits of a certain thoroughbred strain that had its origin in a stud near where I live and he gave me his considered opinion on the matter. He wouldn't take a present of a yearling from that breed, he said: all they produced was aul' strollops. I thought he said trollops, but no; a *strollop*, he explained, was a horse with a lazy, aimless gait in the parade ring.

I had never previously heard this word, and it seems to be confined to the Travellers in Ireland, but I came across it in glossaries from Lancashire. 'A slovenly, untidy walker', says one. Wright's dialect dictionary also has a Lancashire verb *to strollop*: 'To stride or walk about aggressively; to go about in an untidy, slovenly manner.' I wonder is the word to be found elsewhere in Britain. My acquaintance is a good source of rarish words, given his background, but as for his knowledge of blood horses, I have my doubts: Galileo was classified by him as a strollop, and no, he wouldn't breed from him. I have been thinking about the word's origin. My guess is that it's a fusion of *trollop*, ultimately from Old French *troller*, a hunting term meaning to hunt with no purpose, and *stoll*, an early 17th-century borrowing from the High German, introduced by soldiers to Britain. Compare the German *strolch*, a vagabond.

On my last visit to London I heard the word *muss*, a scramble, a free-for-all. I had previously heard the word only once, from a friend, who lives near Lurgan, in Northern Ireland. She remembers the old days when it was customary at society weddings for the groom to fling small coins among the waiting poor at the church door; an unholy muss would ensue.

The great Tudors knew this word. *Musse* was a French game; Randle Cotgrave's French-English dictionary of 1611 gives *musse* as one of the senses of French *mousche*, now *mouche*, a fly. For centuries the dictionaries said that muss came from this game, but the theory has now been discarded; *Oxford* points out that the sense 'scramble' has not been shown to occur in French, and that Cotgrave's explanation was suggested by a similarity of sound in the English word. Percivall's Spanish dictionary of 1591 has '*Rebatina*, scrambling, a musse, a sudden skirmish', precisely today's meaning. A mystery its etymology remains.

As for the verb *to muss*, as used in such as 'he mussed up my hair', this is merely a 19th-century American onomatopoeic alteration of *mess*. But there are other, prettier, musses. *Muss*, the mouth, is still heard in many parts of rural England, I'm told. John Skelton had it in *Speke Parrot* (1529 or thereabouts): 'Goddys blessyng light on thy swete lyttyll mus!' *Muss* was defined by John Florio in his Italian-English dictionary of 1598 as 'a swetehart, a daintie mop'. Both Skelton's and Florio's musses are from Old French *muse*, mouth, muzzle.

The word *gulpin*, which can be both a term of endearment and one of contempt, is common in Scotland, Northumberland, Lincolnshire and Hampshire; and in Ireland only in the province of Ulster. My late wife used gulpin of a young child and of a gullible man. She never heard the word used of a grown woman.

It is from the dialect noun *gulp*, the youngest of any animal in its softest and tenderest state, and this is from *gulp*, to swallow, which has a cognate in the Dutch *gulpen*, to guzzle. The verb has been in English for a considerable time. Langland has *y-gulpid* in *Piers Plowman*.

Gulpin, many dictionaries say, is simply the compound *gulp in*. In British naval circles in the 19th century, a *gulpin* was a marine. *Notes and Queries*, one of academia's most venerable journals, has this from 1867: 'A marine was called a gulpin by the sailors, that is a person who would swallow anything told to him.'

Walter Scott in *St Ronan* has the word *galopin*, a minor servant in a great house, which an American academic recently glossed as being a variant of gulpin. Oh dear. *Galopin* is from French *gallopins*, 'undercooks or scullions in monasteries', according to Cotgrave, mentioned above.

DECEMBER 2001

IN MANY NORTHERN and Midland districts of England, in Scotland and in the north of Ireland too, people *feal* things, whereas you and I would hide them. Nuala Conaghan, who hails from Co. Donegal, but who now lives in Notting Hill in London, wrote to ask about the verb; in her father's farm the hens fealed their eggs in the hay shed, she says; and her mother fealed the sweet Christmas dumplings she made until Christmas morning dawned. The word has been in English literature since 1325, when the anonymous author of one of the Metrical Homilies wrote, 'For his [Christ's] Godhed in fleis was felid.' The word was adopted from the Old Norse *fela*, to hide.

Arthur Hacker, MBE, wrote to me recently from Hong Kong. *Wurrico* was one of his grandmother's words, and he has come across it in both Cornish and Scots invocations. The Scots version goes:

> Frae witches, warlocks an' wurricoes,
> An' evil spirits, an' a' things
> That gang bump i' the nicht
> Good Lord deliver us.

I'm surprised to find the word as far south as Cornwall; the *English Dialect Dictionary* says that it's found only in Scotland and in England's North Country, in various disguises, *worrycow*, *worricow*, *wurricoe* and *wirricow* among them. It defines the word as 'a bugbear; a hobgoblin; any frightful object or awkward-looking person; a scarecrow; the Devil'. Scott, in *The Heart of Midlothian*, has: 'It keeps uncivil folk frae staring as if ane were a worrycow,' and Hogg in his *Tales* speaks of 'the waeful wirricow'.

Now, as to origin we can only guess; and the guess of Mairi Robinson's *Concise Scots Dictionary* is as good as any: from English *worry*, harass, plus *cow*, a Scots word for an object of terror, possibly from English verb *cow*, to intimidate.

When George Macklin from Edinburgh was a young whippersnapper he was wont to shout, 'Bunce!' when he espied another youngster taking a bar of chocolate or some such treat from his satchel at lunchtime. *Bunce*, he tells me, meant that he was making a claim to half of it.

The London version was *bunts*, and it meant profit. Mayhew's *London Labour and the London Poor*, 1851, has, with reference to the haggling done by street urchins, 'All over that amount being the boys' profit or bunts.' In Ulster a *bunce* is a small commission given to a middleman who helps negotiate when a deal seems to be on the verge of collapse. W.H. Patterson's glossary of Antrim and Down words, collected around 1880, connects the word with the flax industry; it defines bunce as 'a consideration in the way of commission given to persons who bring together buyer and seller at a flax market'. *Bunce* is also an Ulster verb, and it means to share money. 'He would not bunce with me' and 'bunce the money' have been recently recorded in Antrim. 'To bunce up', meaning to pool resources for a present, or a meal out, it still common.

But where did the word originate? Nobody knows for sure, and it is regarded as slang nowadays. It is possibly a form of *bonus*, but some have compared the Danish *bundt* and the Swedish *bunt*, words adapted from the German *bund*, a bundle.

Samuel Johnson defined *anecdote* as 'something yet unpublished; a biographical incident; a minute passage of private life'. As for the first meaning, which intrigues Ruth Wharton from Leicester, this is its history. Procopius was general all-round sage at the court of the Roman Emperor Justinian at Constantinople. He died in 562 and might have gone to his reward sooner had his boss found out what he was up to. Apart from writing a book on the Emperor's wars, and another on the many great buildings erected by Justinian, he had, under the bed, a third tome, titled *Anekdota* (Procopius wrote in Greek), meaning 'unpublished things'. They were not published for a very good reason. They contained juicy gossip about the Emperor and his beautiful, mysterious wife Theodora, who, far from being of noble birth, as Justinian had told everybody, was the daughter of a circus bear-tamer, and a former prostitute, according to our sage.

As the old Gaelic storytellers used to say, 'That's my story; if there's a lie in it, so be it; I didn't make it up, I merely retell it.'

I wish you all a happy Christmas.

JANUARY 2002

THE WORD *flipe* is known in the northern half of Ireland, as well as in Scotland and England's North Country. Micheal Traynor's dictionary of Co. Donegal English, compiled in 1955 in Tasmania, would you believe, defines the word as 'an impudent, immoral girl'.

W.F. Marshall was an Ulster dialect poet who published some much-loved light verse in the first half of the last century. A poem in his most famous book, *Livin' in Drumlister*, has the couplet:

> An' the wee back room it wud never do
> For the flipe that was raired in the South.

Towards the middle of the last century, in a novel called *Fardorougha the Miser*, that excellent Ulster novelist William Carleton has a nice gent ask his girlfriend: 'Who made you my mistress, you blaggard flipe?'

I was surprised to find that the *English Dialect Dictionary* has only one Scots entry under this particular *flipe*, and this is from Aberdeen. It seems that the word was used of a man of that part of Scotland, as this quotation from a song published in 1852 proves: 'A good-natured flipe of a husband like me.'

The original meaning of *flipe* was a forehead-cloth worn by women. It is of Scandinavian origin; Danish has *flip*, a protruding piece of shirt, kerchief, etc. In 1530 the important lexicographer Palsgrave has the gloss: 'I tourne up the flepe of a cap.' It seems that the fashionable flepes or flipes, considered saucy and sexy, gave us flipes, women who wore them.

This type of transference is common in many languages. Consider the French *garnement*, defined as (1) *garniture d'habit* and (2) *mauvais sujet*, a bad lot, a ne'er-do-well.

In the Dublin suburb of Ringsend, not long ago a tiny fishing village, I have heard oldies speak of *gibs*, young women without a care in the world. It is not used in any contemptuous sense, a gib is in no sense a flipe.

Where does this word come from? Some say that its origin is *Gilbert*, a medieval name for a favourite cat. *The Romance of the Rose* (c. 1400) is often quoted: 'For right no mo that Gibbe our cat.' The phrase 'to play the gib' was explained in 1566 as 'to act the cat', and used of a wanton woman. But I have a feeling that this gib has nothing to do with cats. In the dictionaries of Lancashire and Lincolnshire I have come across the word, defined as a gosling. The *English Dialect Dictionary* adds, 'figuratively, a young woman whose manners are childish'. As to this gib's origin, I haven't a clue, I'm afraid.

June Forbes from Chesterfield wrote to tell me of her delight in being addressed by another oldie, who manages a street trader's booth, as 'my pigeon'. Is this term of endearment confined to London? she asks.

Well, I can tell you that James Joyce used it in *A Portrait of the Artist as a Young Man*: 'Is that you, pigeon?' And I hear that it is used in many places in England and also in America where the feminist writ does not run. The word was used of a young woman in Tudor times. Greene, in 1592, writing about the thankless people often encountered in this imperfect world, has: 'When they had spent upon her what they had, then forsooth she and her young pigeon [her daughter] turne them out of doores like prodigal children.'

There are only a few references in literature prior to that, but we can be sure that the usage was common since the Middle Ages, when English borrowed *pyjon*, *pejon* from Old French *pyjoun*, a dove, a young bird. From Late Latin *pipio*, a young bird, from Latin *pipere*, to cheep, chirp. An imitative word, this pipere, like the Greek *pipos*, a fledgling, and long, long ago, the Sanskrit *pippaka*, a species of bird whose name was an imitation of its call.

Ducky is still with us as a term of endearment, and it has nothing to do with ducks. Its origin is Old Norse *dokka*, a word that has survived in Modern Danish as *dukke*. It means a doll.

Is chuck still in use outside my native Wexford as a term of endearment, I wonder? My daughter hates the word, even more than she hates ducky. A *chuck* is a chicken, from Old Norse *kjuklingr*. Macbeth addressed his wife as 'dearest chuck'. Some chicken.

FEBRUARY 2002

IN THIS MISERABLE time of the year fetches are seen all over the place, if you can believe some of the oldies. A *fetch*, according to John Banim, a sadly neglected Irish novelist, is:

the supernatural facsimile of some individual, which comes to assure its original, or friend or relative, a happy longevity or immediate dissolution. If seen in the morning the one event is predicted; if in the evening, the other.

Henderson's excellent *Folk Lore* (1879) assures me that the word is not confined to Ireland. I have been making enquiries, and I have been assured that in Shakespeare's district 'Old Fetch will have you' is still used by some oldies as a threat to unruly children. In Pembrokeshire, as well as in my native Wexford, some people are still afraid that they might see the *fetch candle*. This is a supernatural light foretelling the death of the person who sees it. The learned journal *Notes and Queries* had this in 1852: 'The superstition appears in the shape of the fetch candle, a light seen moving in the air at night and supposed to be in attendance on a ghostly funeral, portending the speedy death of the party who sees it.' The journal was referring to Cornwall. I once tried to explain to my grandmother that fetch was methane gas; she gave me the kind of look she would have given me had I denied the existence of the Holy Ghost.

The great dictionaries say that the word is of uncertain origin. For what my humble opinion is worth I think that it may have come from the French *fétiche*, itself from Portuguese *fetico*, a charm, and if I'm right it is related to *fetish*, defined by Collins as something, especially an inanimate object, that is believed in certain cultures to be the embodiment or habitation of a spirit.

Mismarrow is a word you'll find in many dialects of Scotland, northern England and Ulster. 'Don't mismarrow the papers' means don't mix them up. The dialect poet Wallace from Dumfries has this in 'The Schoolmaster', written in 1899:

> O we're a' mismarrowed thegither,
> O we're a' misfitted and wrang.

Mismarrow is also a noun: one of a pair that does not correspond, anything that is wrongly matched, a grey in a team of bay horses for example.

Marrow, noun and verb, from which mismarrow comes, is also well known in Scotland and Ulster, and in England in many dialects south of the border as far as Chester. The noun means a match, equal: an exact counterpart or likeness, a facsimile. 'Mysell for speed had not my marrow,' boasted the great Hogg, while John Clare from Northamptonshire had 'a mon wha's marrow's hard to meet'. *Marrow* can also mean a companion, mate, partner, hence *marrowless*, companionless, solitary, unmarried. A child's rhyme from Cheshire goes:

> The robin and the wren
> Are God's cock and hen,
> The martin and the swallow
> Are God's mate and marrow.

In Co. Antrim the verb has been defined as 'to lend men or horses to a neighbour and to receive a similar loan in return when needed'.

Of obscure origin. *Oxford*, careful as always, says:

> The localities would seem to point to a Scandinavian origin, but no possible Scandinavian source is known, unless indeed the sense of the English noun can have been developed from that of Old Norse *margr* 'many', friendly, communicative.

I can tell Barbara Holden from Henley that *doily* is named after a London linendraper who lived in the mid- or late 17th century over his shop in the Strand. The *Spectator* had this to say about him in 1712: 'The famous Doiley is still fresh in everyone's memory, who raised a fortune by finding out materials for such stuffs as might at once be cheap and genteel.'

Swift knew a doily as a napkin used after dinner, when slobbers came into their own. In his *Journal to Stella* for 23 April 1711, he has:

'After dinner we had coarse Doily-napkins, fringed at the end, upon the table to drink with.'

John Betjeman speaks of them in 'A Few Late Chrysanthemums': 'Beg pardon, I'm soiling the doileys with afternoon tea and scones.' That was written in 1954. Yesterday I asked a local young one what a doily was. She had no idea. Will the word soon be marked 'obsolete' in the dictionaries?

MARCH 2002

ONE OF THE PLEASURES of working in the world of words in the possibility of finding a connection between words that at first glance don't appear to be remotely related. I was reminded of this the other night as I spoke to a carpenter friend of mine about the tools of his trade. The word *auger* came up. There is, would you believe, a connection between auger and that part of the anatomy called the navel or belly button. How come? The belly button is not bored by an obstetrician's auger, after all.

Well, the Old English *nafela*, navel, is a close relative of the Old English *nafu*, nave. The nave is the hub from which the spokes of the wheel radiate, and through which a hole is bored to fit the axle. (This nave is not the same word as the nave of a church, by the way. The ecclesiastical *nave* is from Latin *navem*, accusative of *navis*, a ship.) In Old English a compound was formed from *nafu* and *gar*, a spear, to give a name to the tool used to make the hole in the nave or hub of a wheel. This new word was *nafogar*. In Middle English this word eventually came to be spelled *nauger*, and then in the 15th century a *nauger* was incorrectly divided as *an auger*, the tool my carpenter friend uses to bore holes in wood.

Shakespeare had *nave* for navel. 'Brave Macbeth ... ne'er shook hands, nor bade farewell to him, Till he unseamed him from the nave to the chaps.'

The prefix *mis-*, from Old English *mis-*, or, in borrowed words, from Old French *mes-* or from Old High German *missi-*, *missa-*, has given the dialects of English some extraordinary words. I've collected some further samples of them for you. Some of them have found their way abroad; some have never left home but are found in dialect stories and poems, and, of course, in the scores of dialect dictionaries that were produced in the 19th century. I wonder how many of them have survived the onslaught of modernity.

Misgraft is a Sussex word. It means mistaken: 'Ye be misgraft about that.'

Misbeholden is an adjective found in Scotland and in northern England. It is generally used of speech, and it means offensive, ill-natured, out of place in civilized company.

Misboden was common in the 19th century in Newcastle-upon-Tyne – for all I know it is still in use there – and it means injured. Chaucer has, 'Or who hath you misboden?' in *The Canterbury Tales*. This is from Old English *misbéoden*, to ill-use.

Miscarriage should be used with a degree of caution by Scots and Yorkshire people, I'm told. For instance, 'I'm sorry about your miscarriage,' means simply, 'I'm sorry you have had bad luck.' That could easily be misconstrued, or *misconstere*, as was said in Lancashire.

Stevenson wrote *misconvenient* for inconvenient; I've heard this in many places in eastern Ireland.

To *misdoubt* means to disbelieve in many places in both Scotland and Ulster. 'I don't misdoubt you,' my late wife, an Ulster woman, used to say.

Does *misgo* still survive in Kent and Somerset? I heard it years ago in Donegal as *misgae*, which is a Scots pronunciation. It means to go wrong, to go astray. 'Her was oncommon nice maid; 'tis a thousand pities her should a miswent,' was recorded in Somerset.

To *mislear* in both Scotland and Ulster means to misinform, to lead astray, to seduce. The English of Wexford once has the noun *mizlear*, a dangerous fly-boy. The verb, and, I suppose, the Wexford noun, are from the Old English *misloeran*, to teach wrongly, to persuade a person to do what is wrong.

A word of thanks to all who wrote to me about *flipe/flype*, especially to 83-year-old Mrs Flora Isserlis from Edinburgh. R.M. Milne of Perth tells me that flype, apart from meaning to fold back, to turn inside out, can also mean to tear off skin in strips, to peel.

As a gloss Mr Milne offers this story. Two Scots farm labourers were discussing the relative beauty of their wives. 'Your Jean is so very ugly,' said one. 'Ah, but she's all glorious within,' said the other. 'Pity you can't flype her,' was the reply.

APRIL 2002

HELLO SAILORS! Mr W. Tyson of Allithwaite, Granger-Over-Sands, Cumbria and Mr Leo Carthy of Lady's Island, Co. Wexford, Ireland, want your help in connection with two phrases used by seamen. Mr Tyson is intrigued by *Jacob's Join*, which was common in the British navy in his day. It was used, he tells me, 'to describe a meal to which all the diners contributed a dish of food, and all the diners ate what they wanted from whatever dishes they fancied'. There is no difficulty with the word *join*. It was a communal meal, or street party, to which people contributed food or drink, but where does *Jacob* fit in? Mr Carthy's phrase is *cap and jury*. This is a huge rogue wave that strikes a boat broadside on as she attempts to beat against a storm. My correspondent heard the word from Irish lifeboatmen. Over to you, ye mariners of England.

Michelle Henry from Dover wrote to ask if I would agree that the spelling of English should be reformed given that it is a notoriously unreliable guide to pronunciation, and asks why American spelling differs from ours. Well, many attempts have been made to reform our spelling, none of them very successful, and I feel that we should leave well enough alone. As to why the Americans have gone their own sweet way, Noah Webster (1758–1843) was mainly responsible. A Yale-trained lawyer, Noah wrote *A Grammatical Institute of the English Language*, in which was incorporated *The American Spelling Book*, in which he sought to free American English from dependence on British models of the standard language. A true patriot. In 1806 he published *A Compendious Dictionary*, but most of the reforms he advocated in this work were dropped because of the fierce opposition of Emerson, among others. In his famous *American Dictionary of the English Language* (1828) Webster modified his stance on spelling, but here we have for the first time *honor*, *center*, *defense*; and *public* instead of the then standard *publick*. His insistence that educated American usage should be regarded as standard was a great advance, patriotic Americans such as Benjamin Franklin and that notoriously bad speller, George Washington, agreed. Webster was beaten to the punch by a John Barry in entering the first American-published book for copyright. This Barry did in Philadelphia on 9 June 1790. The book's title was *The Philadelphia Spelling Book*.

And who was this John Barry? None other than the Wexfordman who became the first commissioned officer of the fledgling American navy to capture an enemy ship, the first commodore of his navy, and the man regarded as its father. I'm afraid, though, that John Barry's attempt at reforming spelling was as crackpot as the attempts made on this side of the ocean, including those of Shaw and the Simplified Spelling Society. As late as 1948, the distinguished dialectologist Harold Orton recommended a new spelling system. Thank God, nobody listened to them. Consider this effort, and breathe a sigh of relief: 'We rekwier dhe langgwej as an instrooment; we mae aulsoe study its history. Dhe presens ov reprezenting dhe seam leter; aul dhis for eusez ov dhe seam leter; aul dhis for uesez ov dhe value of a langgwej az an instrooment ...'

Just because one word resembles another does not mean that they are related. Take *pest* and *pester*, asked about by Ruth Hodges from Canterbury. In the days of Elizabeth I English borrowed the word *peste* from French, which had borrowed it from Latin *pestis*. This was a very serious pest indeed, bubonic plague. In time, as the fear of the plague receded, any troublesome person or thing became a pest. Now take the verb *pester*. This ultimately comes from the Latin *pastor*, a shepherd. The French got to work on the word in the Middle Ages. Their *empestere* meant to spancel an animal, as shepherds sometimes have to do, and so to impede. It came by way of *pastoria*, found in the Latin of early German law: a spancel for a horse. *Empestrer* was borrowed into English in the 16th century as *pester*. First it meant to impede, but soon, because people thought it must be related to *pest*, it acquired the meaning 'nuisance'. A tricky business, this etymology.

MAY 2002

'For women are crabbed, that comes them of kynde.' Words taken, my dear brethren, from one of the York Mysteries, *c.* 1400. *Crabbed* is an adjective that survived in many dialects of Britain and Ireland; in describing a person it means cantankerous, perverse. A common variant is *crabbit*. Hazel Brooke of Notting Hill, London, wrote to ask if the word is related to the fruit of the wild apple tree, a sour, harsh, tart, astringent fruit. She finds that her dictionary says that the word is related to crab, the crustacean.

A darlin' question. From the beginning of the 16th century the Scots had the form *scrab*, a word of Norse origin, for the crab apple. In some Modern Swedish dialects this still survives as *skrabba*. This was most probably a transferred sense of the Old English *crabba* or Old Norse *krabbi*, the crustacean.

The primary reference was to the crooked or wayward gait of the crustacean, and the contradictory, perverse and fractious disposition that this expressed, according to *Oxford*. The Germans have *krabbe*, and according to the great grammarian Grimm, who also wrote frightening fairy tales with his brother, it exists 'because these animals are malicious and do not easily let go when they are seized'. Fair enough. Low German and East Frisian also have *krabbe*, a crab, and by transference, a cantankerous man.

Crab is also a verb. It means to find fault with, to make little of somebody or something. I have come across this in Ulster and in the language of the Travellers. In that great glossary of Antrim and Down words published by W.H. Patterson in 1890 we find: 'A couldn't thole [endure<Old English *tholian*] bein' crabbed at, when A didn't do nothin' ondaicent.' A member of the Connors clan of Travellers told me not long ago about his efforts to sell a mare to a member of another clan: 'He went too far crabbin' the mare, boss, so I told him to fuck off.'

I have heard yet another *crab*, a verb meaning to scratch, in both the north of Ireland and in Cornwall. It's probably in many other dialects as well. It is related to crab the crustacean, and it's the same word as the Low German *krabben*, to scrape, scratch.

In English, *to crab* was originally a hawking term. *The Sportsman's Diary* of 1785 tells us that hawks are prone to crab when they stand too close to one another. Turbeville's *Faulconrie* of 1575 also has the word: 'Some falcons will crabbe with every hawk and flee of purpose to crabbe with them.' That comes of kynde, I suppose.

A physician friend of mine has a very interesting collection of gruesome medieval prints relating to his profession. As he proudly gave me a private viewing recently he asked me, in relation to a picture of a surgeon, surrounded by his pupils, examining a patient's eye that he had pulled or pushed out about half an inch from where it was supposed to be, if there was an etymological relationship between pupil, the part of the eye, and the word that means student.

There is indeed. To the ancient Romans the word *pupa* meant a little girl or doll. Now no doubt you will have, gentle reader, many's the time and oft looked into somebody's eyes in a moment of romantic bliss and seen there a miniature of yourself. The Romans, being rather fond of these longing, lingering gazes – think of Catullus and Dean Martin – called the opening of the iris in which the image is seen *pupilla*; the beholder sees himself in his darling's eyes as her little doll, you understand. So far so good?

Now an orphaned girl was also called *pupilla*; an orphaned boy *pupillus*. In Middle French and in Middle English one word, *pupille*, served both sexes. When the word first reached England in the 14th century it had the old Roman meaning of an orphaned child looked after by others. Two centuries later the meaning had changed somewhat; a *pupil* was now a child looked after by a school or a private schoolmaster. Thus our two English pupils, with two different meanings, have the Latin *pupa*, girl, doll as their ultimate origin. Such is the way of words.

JUNE 2002

AIDEN TURNER–BISHOP of Preston, Lancashire, may have solved the problem of *Jacob's Join*, I feel. He writes:

> I don't know about the phrase being a maritime expression, because it is certainly alive in Lancashire and north-west England. Our office 'do' in the Library of the University of Central Lancashire, Preston, last year, was a Jacob's Join. Members of the staff each brought in some cheese, wine, pastries, etc.

Mr Turner-Bishop also sent me copies of advertisements that show that our troublesome phrase survives in Lancashire outside Preston. 'You are warmly invited to our Jacob's Join,' says a Clitheroe Salvation Army advertisement; and in a speech to the Ashton-in-Makerfield Co-operative Women's Guild, Mrs Wilson, its secretary, quoted from the first Minute Book (1906), telling us that the then-secretary Mrs Button devised a competition for which the entrance fee was one halfpenny, consisting of a buttonhole competition, a Jacob's Join and a Cobweb Special, whatever that is. My correspondent suggests that a Jacob's Join stems from Genesis 31:46. 'And Jacob said unto his brethren, gather stones; and they took stones, and made a heap; and they did eat there upon the heap.'

Mrs Henrietta Wilson wrote from Glasgow about the good word *spreet*. I heard the word for the first time last year. A man from Co. Antrim who had ventured south with his family used it in reference to his young son who crash-landed on to a restaurant table while imitating an out-of-control Spitfire. Antrim people also refer to a bantam as a *spreet of a hen* and call a Jack Russell a *spreet of a dog*. The word is a variant of *sprite*, itself from the Old French *esprite*, spirit, from Latin *spiritus*.

A relative of mine who lives in Cornwall tells me that *spreet* is used as a verb there, and in Devon also. It means to haunt a person after death. One of my dialect dictionaries quotes a female oldie from Penzance frightening children: 'I'll come back when I'm dead an' spreet ee.' Hence their word *spreety*, ghostly. *To spreet* also means to wander about. The *English Dialect Dictionary* quotes a Cornish landlady laying down the law to a guest: 'I don't like people staying with me spreeting from room to room before I'm up.'

Mary D'Arcy, a Dublin woman, wrote to ask if there is a connection between *hobby-horse* and *hobby*, a favourite pastime.

There is. First of all, a *hobby* in the Middle Ages was a small, tough horse. It became a child's name for a horse, and afterwards, around Shakespeare's time, it became a name for a toy horse. Not long afterwards both hobby and hobby-horse became offensive terms, 'said of a woman who romps with me', as the *EDD* put it; and 'to make a hobby of oneself' means to behave foolishly, in both Co. Tipperary and Yorkshire.

In Padstow in Cornwall on May Day a hobby-horse was carried through the streets to a pool a mile out of town. The head was dropped into the pool, and the water sprinkled on the spectators.

The procession used to return home singing a song to commemorate the tradition that the French, who landed in the bay, mistook a party of mummers in red cloaks for soldiers, and fled hell-for-leather to their boats.

The etymology is interesting. The Middle English was *hoby*; the Old French *hobin, hobi, haubby*, whence Modern French *aubin* and Italian *ubino*. But the Old French was adapted from the English and was a variant of *Robin* or *Robbie*, a pet-name for a horse. Once upon a time *hoby* was a generic name for an Irish-bred horse. A tract of 1400 describes 'an lyrysche man Uponne his hoby'. Another by-form of the same name, *dobbin*, has become a generic name for a cart-horse.

My thanks to Mr Bill Blackett of Rottingdean, Brighton and Dr John Griffin of Cullompton, Devon for very valuable word-lists. I remember Ted Hughes saying:

> Whatever other speech you grow into, presumably your dialect stays alive in a sort of inner freedom ... it's your childhood self there inside the dialect and that is possibly your real self or the core of it ... Without it, I doubt if I would ever have written verse.

Thank God for English dialects.

JULY 2002

I WAS SURPRISED recently to be sent the word *tallamacka* by Mrs Hilary Morton from Penrith in Cornwall, whose mother used it many years ago in such notices of intent as, 'I'll raise tallamacka if I find you haven't behaved while I'm out.' I can't find the word in any of the dialects of England and I had assumed that it was confined to Ireland. Its origin baffled me.

Back in 1998 I asked for help about the word here in *The Oldie*. I got only one reply, from Rev. B.H. Sharp of Cymbach, near Aberdare. For some reason I didn't publish his letter, which was very remiss of me. At any rate, here it is now for the benefit of my Cornish reader:

> Would tallamacka have a religious connection? St Telemachos (his Greek name; he is Almachius in Roman Catholic calendars) was martyred in Rome about 400 AD. He was a monk from the East who sought to put an end to gladiatorial contests. One day he ran into the arena to separate the contestants. There was a riot and poor Telemachos was killed in the affray. Nobody is sure who killed him. Perhaps it was the mob who didn't want their fun ruined; perhaps it was the gladiators on the order of the city prefect, who thought such unruly scenes bad for business. Anyway, it is said that as a result of the affray the emperor Honorius abolished such barbarous shows. Did the saint give his name to the uproar?

Well, what do you think?

Last week I had occasion to buy a present for a young lady of the accountancy persuasion who sorted out a problem for me. I chose perfume, a Parisian delight called Joy, which I can recognize across a crowded room and which cost an arm and two legs. I was surprised by the nice card I got thanking me for the lovely scent. *Scent!* Scent was what we called the inexpensive stuff we bought at Christmas for the young ones a lifetime ago when twenty seemed like old age; I had thought the word had since fallen on hard times until a little research revealed that is has made a big comeback in America, where it is being used once more in the grander shops on Fifth Avenue instead of perfume, parfum and fragrance.

Interesting words, all of these. Once upon a time *scent* meant any kind of strong smell. Caxton, back in 1410, wrote about 'the sente and savour of the dede man'. The word wasn't applied to a liquid perfume until the 18th century. The word can be traced to the Latin *sentire*, to feel, which found its way into French as *sentir*, to feel, to smell. In Middle English it became *sent*.

Perfume and the French *parfum* became the in word for expensive concoctions when Mme Coco Chanel rejected as unworthy of her Chanel No. 5 such a plebian word as scent. This was the very first perfume to be made completely from chemicals. Perfume is from an old Italian word *perfumare*, from *par*, through and *fumare*, to smoke, as happens, for example, when priests send out the smoke of incense from a thurible. The word came to France in due course as *parfumer*, and they made a noun *parfum* that the English borrowed in the 16th century.

What's the connection with smoke? A herbal written in 1533 tells us. It shows that burning was the means of releasing the fragrance from herbs: 'I take for a parfum the ryndes of old rosemary and burn them.' This burning was done for many reasons. Juniper berries were burned in a room in an attempt to fumigate it during the plague; 17th-century physicians told people to burn flower petals to cure a cold; and people thought of burning sweet-smelling flowers to release their perfume.

Fragrance, from Old French *fragrance*, from Late Latin *fraganti*, is now as commonly used as perfume. Milton would be pleased. He was the first to use the word in literature, in *Paradise Lost*, where he speaks of Eve 'veiled in a cloud of fragrance'. Joy, by Jean Patou de Paris: now that would have been ideal.

AUGUST 2002

AN IRISH WOMAN living in Cheshire, too shy to have her name mentioned in *The Oldie*, wrote to me a while ago asking about what she considers to be the ignorant way in which the word *ax* is used instead of *ask* by Irish people, in such phrases as 'he axed me out'. She could have said, by people all over the English speaking world who use the dialect, Cheshire included; ax has survived all the attempts of schooling to eradicate it.

Well, although ax is now considered a vulgarism it has as long a pedigree as ask. 'I am often axed to tell it, sire,' says a character in Crofton Croker's *Fairy Legends and the Traditions of the South of Ireland* (1862). The sentence surprisingly drew a friendly admonition from young Tennyson, who, twenty years later, in one of his ventures into the field of dialect poetry, himself wrote this as an example of the speech of Lincolnshire: 'Summun 'ed hax'd fur a son, and 'e promised a son to shee.' 'Axe, and it shall be geven you,' was Tindale's 1526 translation of Matthew 7:7. 'How shold I axen mercy of Tisbe?' axed Chaucer in *The Legend of Good Women*. Wyclif, in 1388, wrote, 'Whanne he schal axe, what shal Y answere to hym?'

Ax is from the Old English *ácsian*, to ask. The result of the Old English metathesis *asc-*, *acs-*, was that Middle English had the types ax and ask among others. Down to about 1600 ax, found mostly in southern England, was the common literary form, thereafter ask became more accepted, although ax probably remained the norm in childhood.

The phrase *to ask the banns* is found in Middle English to this day. It means to publish the banns of marriage. Up to recent days to be *out-axed* in Kent meant to have your marriage banns called for the last time. In Cork a young woman of sixteen or so is considered *axable*, that is old enough to be asked to marry or, as is often the case nowadays, I'm told, asked to bed without benefit of clergy.

Unrelated asks: in parts of Scotland an *ask* is the stake to which a cow is tethered in the cow-house. This is from the Old Norse *askr*, the ash tree. *Ask* is also applied to things made of ash, such as wooden dishes in Shetland and Orkney. In Norse myth Ask was the first man, created by God from the ash tree. One final *ask*. This is a Co. Carlow word for a newt. I've not heard of it elsewhere in Ireland. It's from the Old English *athexe*, a lizard.

Felicity MacDermott now lives in Ireland, but she was born and reared on Exmoor, where she heard the verb *to lear*. She is slightly confused about this verb because it has two different meanings. She writes:

The new owner of a sheep farm with grazing on the moor always bought in a portion of his predecessor's sheep because they were leared, and would not stray. But an old farmer for whom I worked once used to say never travel leary, in other words, find a return load for your cart. Different words?

Yes, they are. The first *lear* is from Old English *loeran*, to teach. It is still alive and well in Scotland, in the northern counties, and in southern England. *Leer-father* is a Yorkshire word for an exemplar, one whose conduct influences others. The other *lear*, unladen, is from Middle English *lere*, empty. The *English Dialect Dictionary* tells me that it is found in most English counties and that it has spawned *lear-headed*, empty-headed; *lear-handed*, empty-handed; *learness*, emptiness. *Lear* can also mean hungry, thin, meagre from hunger. I've heard the word, meaning empty, in my own county, Wexford.

For John Ennis of Fulham: the English dialect word *cant*, a cut of meat, a slice of bread, gave the Irish *cannta*, not the other way round. The English word is itself a borrowing from Middle Dutch *kant*, a piece or portion. It's in Sanskrit as *khanda*, and that's as far back as I can go.

SEPTEMBER 2002

CANDY, as all the world knows since Ogden Nash proclaimed it so in his 'Reflections on Ice-breaking', is dandy, but liquor is quicker. By *candy* Mr Nash meant chocolates; on this side of the Atlantic the word means boiled sweets, and although I am no expert on these matters, a proffered paper bag of bull's-eyes wouldn't, I fancy, get a fellow very far nowadays. I write about the word now because I see it here in front of me in a list of proscribed goodies sent to a friend of mine who has been diagnosed as having diabetes 2.

A long history candy has. In Sanskrit the term used for large lumps of sugar was *khanda sakara*. *Khanda* meant a piece, and it came from the root *khand*, to break up. It travelled from India to Persia, and from Persian the Arab traders got their *sukkar quandi*, a term that eventually gave the French *sucre candi* in the 14th century. It came here as sugar candy and the sugary candy of the nursery rhyme. It wasn't until the 18th century that people dropped the adjective, leaving the noun to fend for itself.

The Sanskrit *sakara* originally meant gravel; the sweet stuff has gritty crystals. The Persians borrowed the word as *shakar*, and the Arabs borrowed it from the Persians as *sukkar*. The Crusaders loved this exotic sweetener; up to then honey was used all over Europe. The trouble with sukkar was that it was very expensive; the Venetian traders made vast fortunes from it and its price didn't drop until Columbus proved that it would grow in abundance outside the Middle East. Sukkar became *succarum* and *zuccarum* in Medieval Latin. From there it passed into Italian as *zuccero*, and eventually it reached English by way of Old French *sukere* and *zuchre*.

As I mentioned briefly last month, the Sanskrit word *khand*, a bit, piece, brought to mind the English dialect word *cant*, a cut or joint of meat, a slice of bread. William Cobbett used the word, I remember, and I'm told that it is still in use in many southern and Midland dialects. In Irish we have *canta*, a borrowing from the English word, itself borrowed from the Middle Dutch *kant*, 'a piece, a portion, a district of land, a piece of bread', according to Verdam, the great authority on these matters. The Dutch word can be traced all the way back to ancient India.

'In my young days,' writes John Baird of Bangor, 'a bogey in golf was what we now call a par. Nowadays a bogey is one over par. Why is this, and what is the origin of bogey anyway?'

An article written in 1908 has this:

> One popular song has left its permanent effect on the game of

golf. That song is 'The Bogey Man'. In 1890 Dr Thomas Browne RN, the honorary secretary of the Great Yarmouth Golf Club, was playing a Major Wellman, the match being played against 'the ground score', which was the name given to the scratch value of each hole. The system of playing was new to Major Wellman, and he exclaimed, thinking of the song of the moment, that his mysterious and well-nigh invincible opponent was a regular 'bogey-man'. The name caught on at Great Yarmouth, and to-day bogey is one of the most feared opponents on all the courses that acknowledge him.

The Americans began to use bogey for one over par in 1898. In S.B. Flexner's *Listening to American* (1982) we are told that 'When the rubber ball replaced the gutta-percha type the British lowered their bogies by one stroke per hole and kept the term; but the Americans began to use par instead, keeping the old British word bogey to mean the old, easier expected score of a good player, usually one stroke more than the new par.'

The change deleted one figurative meaning of the word from our language. A good example of what I mean is to be found in this exchange from P.G. Wodehouse's *The Clicking of Cuthbert* (1922): 'Weren't you giving yourself rather a large family?' 'Was I? I don't know. What's bogey?'

Origin? Perhaps the dialect *bogle* or *boggle*, a phantom causing terror, whose origin may be Welsh *bwg*, ghost, bugbear. But there are German words of similar form, such as *boggel-mann*, our bogey-man, so that uncertainty remains.

OCTOBER 2002

YOU MAY HAVE SEEN the television pictures of the harrowing scenes as the bodies of a grandfather, father and son were brought ashore in a secluded south Wexford cove recently, victims of a tragic fishing accident. That particular coastline was known in the old days of sail as the Graveyard of a Thousand Ships, and in winter you may watch with awe, as I have often done, some of the most frightening seas you'll find this side of Cape Horn running between the Black Rock and Carnsore Point, where the Irish Sea meets the Atlantic. On one of my excursions to this lonely place last winter I called into one of my favourite watering holes, the Lobster Pot, for something warm, and was greeted by an old salt who said to me, 'Hefty weather, ain't it?' Now this district I speak of was famous in linguistic circles for its retention until the middle of the 19th century of an English dialect that Chaucer would have felt at home in, and when I looked up the word *hefty* I found that it is not the word that means 'heavy', a late derivative of 'heave', but an obsolete form from the Dutch *heftigh*, violent. The related German is *heftig*. I am constantly surprised by the English of that part of Ireland.

Paddy MacDonald of Greenwich, New South Wales, is interested in small boats of all kinds, and he has put on a display of Irish boats in the National Maritime Museum in Sydney. He was, he tells me, besieged by people who wanted to know something about those frail craft so often mentioned by Synge in his writings, currachs, or curraghs, long, narrow rowing-boats of tarred canvas stretched over laths of timber and used by the fishermen of Ireland and Scotland since auld lang syne. All this expert wanted from me was the etymology of *currach*. The word is from Irish *curach*, a little ship; Scots Gaelic borrowed it from us. Compare the Welsh *corwg*, also *corwgl* and *cwrwgl*, and of course *coracle*. These point to an Old Celtic unattested word, *kurug-os*, boat. The word was introduced into English by St Cuthbert, who wrote in a 1450 tract: 'Thai called their bate a currok.'

Years ago, when I was engaged in the academic life, I was asked to accompany a bevy of beauties from a Florida university to the Aran Island of Inishmore. Five of them accompanied me and our ageing oarsman out in a currach to fish for mackerel. About a mile from shore, with the mackerel ignoring us, my five 18-year-olds decided to strip naked and slip over the side to race back to the beach. You may imagine my shock, gentle readers, as some of the hussies showed their expertise in the backstroke. My old boatman kept saying various prayers and incantations in Irish at the top of his voice, as he tried to keep pace with them, and I'm assured that he told of the famous swim in the local pubs until the day he died. One of the girls afterwards won an Olympic gold medal for the United States, and she sent old O'Flaherty, the currachman, and me autographed photographs as a memento.

The old northern English and Scots verb *to kemp*, to strive for mastery, could not, I think, be used of my American swimming ladies, as it is (should I say 'was'?) used exclusively of farm labourers. I heard the word in Ulster in the sixties, but a lot of changes have overtaken the farmers' world since then and it may now be obsolete there. A 19th-century treasury of British lore has:

> It was common for the reapers on the last day to have a contention for superiority in quickness of dispatch, groups of three or four taking each a ridge, and striving which should soonest get to its termination. In Scotland this was called a kemping.

Judith Ross of Aberdeen asked about the word, which she found in Scott's *Nigel* (1822).

It's from Middle English *kempen*, related to Middle Dutch *kempen, kimpen*, and Old Norse *kempa*. The first sighting of kemp in literature is in *Le Morte Arthur* (c. 1420): 'There es no kynge undire Criste may kempe with hym one.'

NOVEMBER 2002

NOT LONG AGO at a dinner party in London town I met the delicious Miss Janet Adams from Belfast, who asked me if I was familiar with the term pillow-bere. The word was new to me and she went on to explain that a pillow to me was a *pillow-bere* to her. Her friend, a Mr Ken Prince from Barnsley, piped up. A *pillow-bere* where he came from was a pillowcase or slip, but he remembered some Yorkshire oldies using the word for a bolster. I promised to look into the matter and here is the result of my consumption of gallons of midnight oil.

A pillow-bere is a pillow slip in parts of England's North Country, in Lincolnshire, Shropshire, East Anglia and in the south-western counties. The oldest reference I could find is in the inventory of Owlsbury Manor House in Shropshire for 1625: 'Eight pair of flaxen pillow beare, one coarse pillow beare.' I also found that the Antrim definition was justified; Wright's great dialect dictionary confirms this. In many Scottish glossaries it is defined as 'a pillow'. To give Mr Prince his due, Wright has 'pillow-bere: a bolster', from Yorkshire.

An old word this is. Chaucer has, 'Ne was ther swich snother Pardoner For in his male he hadde a pilwe beer, Which that he sayde, was our lady veyl.' He also spelled the word 'bere': 'Many a pillow and every bere Of cloth of Raines to slepe on soft.' Thomas Hood was the last writer of note to use the word. In 1850 he wrote: 'Right beautiful the dewy meads appear … What then, if I prefer my pillow-beer?'

Bere is Common Teutonic in origin. The Middle English is *bere* or *beer*, cognate with Low German *büre*, adapted in Modern German as *bühre*. Of obscure origin. *Pillow* comes ultimately from the Latin *pulvinus*, a cushion, a word adapted by the Germans as early as the 2nd century AD, and which slipped into Anglo-Saxon as *pyle* and *pylu*.

I gave up cigarettes recently, but I must confess that I still have a terrible yen for them. I mentioned this to a friend the other day and she replied helpfully, 'Yen. Now where does that come from?' *Yen* is a strong desire, and the word came to us via the USA from China. In the middle of the 19th century many Chinese who smoked opium made their way to America and they brought their Cantonese *yan*, a craving, with them. Those who spoke Mandarin would have said *yin* or *ying*. *Oxford* reminds us that those poor people who built America's railroads also had the words *yin* in Cantonese and *yan* in Mandarin for opium itself. At all events the slightly altered yen was soon used in America to describe any strong desire. It seems to have reached our shores before 1880.

Jennifer Hutchinson from Dublin's Sandymount has, like myself, a yen for Italian food. She would like to know the origin of some Italian culinary words, and suggests that a note on the history of the various dishes would be nice on restaurant menus. A good idea, methinks, even though a fastidious diner might not like to be reminded that his or her *vermicelli*, a pasta dish made from strings thinner than spaghetti, derives from *vermicello*, a diminutive of *verme*, a worm, from Latin *vermis*.

Ziti is a tubular pasta very much in evidence at marriage feasts in the south of Italy. *Ziti* is the plural of an obsolete word for a boy, *zito*. The reason for its appearance at weddings is thought to be its phallic shape. *Spaghetti* is plural of *spaghetto*, diminutive of *spago*, a string. *Pasta* comes from the Late Latin *pasta*, dough, paste. *Lasagna* is named from the ancient Roman *lasanum*, a cooking pot. *Ravioli* is from Italian *rava*, which comes from the Latin *rapa*, and it means 'small turnip'. *Ditali* or *ditalini* I've eaten in those lovely intimate little restaurants you'll find in the side streets of Florence; this is macaroni cut into short pieces shaped like a *ditale*, a thimble.

My favourite among Jennifer's list are *capellitti*, cases of dough filled with meat or cheese. From Medieval Latin *capellus*, a hat or cap, and absolutely delicious.

DECEMBER 2002

SOME TIME AGO an Irish priest wrote to me about the word lewd, which his mother used in the phrase 'to be lewd of oneself'. *Lewd* to most of us means obscene, but to this old lady it meant something else entirely; 'you should be lewd of yourself' meant 'you should be ashamed of yourself'. This meaning was once very common in my native county, Wexford, and Patrick Kennedy, a respected 19th-century folklorist, has this in his *Fireside Stories*, published in 1870: 'And didn't the poor fellows [then] look very lewd of themselves.' I have failed to find this meaning of lewd in any of the dialect glossaries of England. Perhaps it lurks somewhere in deepest Devon, Dorset or Cornwall, dialects that have a lot in common with the dialects of south-eastern Ireland.

At any rate, what an extraordinary history this word lewd has. The meaning unchaste, obscene, is a development of the original meaning of the word, and dates from Chaucer's time; in the prologue to 'The Miller's Tale' he has: 'Læt be thy lewed dronken harlotrye.'

The origin of lewd in its many shades of meaning is the Anglo-Saxon *læwede*, a word now thought to be unconnected to the Latin *laicus*, though that's precisely what *læwede* means: not in holy orders, not clerical. In 1380 Wyclif was writing about lay brothers, *lewid freris*, who said 'four and twenti pater nostris for matynes'. Another development was the meaning unlearned, unlettered; a tract from around 1225 spoke of *lewede* men who didn't understand

Latin. Then it took on the meaning common, low, vulgar, belonging to the lower orders. 'The Miller's Tale' has: 'Ye men shul been as lewed as gees.' It also had the meaning bad, worthless, which survived until Shakespeare's time. My correspondent's meaning is, I feel, a development of that second meaning of Chaucer's.

Christmas is upon us. Have you made the *kissing bunch* yet? Or hung up the *kissing bush*? If you don't know what these items are, the chances are you're not from either Derbyshire or the North Country. I came upon an account of the former in that venerable learned journal, *Notes and Queries*. This was written in 1877:

> This [Derbyshire] kissing bunch is always an elaborate affair. The size depends on the couple of hoops – one thrust through the other – which forms its skeleton. Each of the ribs is garlanded with holly, ivy, and sprigs of other greens, with bits of coloured ribbon and paper roses, rosy-cheeked apples, and oranges. Three small dolls are also prepared, and these represent Our Saviour, the mother of Jesus, and Joseph. These dolls generally hang within the kissing bunch, by strings from the top, and are surrounded by apples and oranges tied to strings, and various coloured ornaments. Occasionally these dolls are arranged in the kissing bunch to represent a manger scene. Generally a bit of mistletoe is obtainable and this is carefully tied to the bottom of the kissing bunch, which is then hung in the middle of the house-place.

Kissing bushes were made all over England in the old days. In Devon they consisted of small furze bushes, dipped in water, powdered with flour and studded all over with holly berries. Every time a kiss was taken, a berry was plucked from the bush. Have these old customs survived anywhere, I wonder?

Christmas always reminds me of an Irish poet called Bláthmac who flourished 1250 years ago. He wrote a series of beautiful poems about the Nativity in Old Irish. They have retained their freshness and fragrance even in translation. Addressing a petition to the Virgin he says that it is her son's hand that has strewn in the firmament the gaming-board of beautiful stars. His petition is a simple one; he wants to live to be an oldie:

> Beautiful Mary, little bright-necked one,
> Get me, sun of women, from your son,
> The blessing that I be in this world till very old with the Lord who rules starry Heaven,
> And that thereafter there be a welcome from me into the everlasting kingdom.

Happy Christmas to all.

JANUARY 2003

THEY TELL ME that the slang word *swank*, noun, verb and adjective, and the adjective *swanky* are becoming obsolete. Posh has taken over, and I must say that Swanky Spice would not suit the young lady at all. No. There is a strutting, swinging air about swanky, something slightly vulgar, or so I feel.

The noun has the meaning 'ostentatious or pretentious behaviour or talk; swagger, pretence', according to *Oxford*. It came into general English slang from an old dialect word found in the Midlands and in the south-west. It was first noted in print in Baker's Northamptonshire glossary of 1844: 'Swank: an ostentatious air, an affectation of stateliness in the walk. What a swank he cuts.'

The noun came from the verb. The etymological meaning is uncertain, but perhaps the original motion is that of a swinging in the body; this would mean that the word is ultimately related to Old High German and Middle High German *swanc*, swinging motion, and to Middle High German *swanken* (Modern German *schwanken*), to sway or totter. The first mention of the verb in English is in a Bedfordshire dialect dictionary of 1809, which gives *swangk*, to strut.

Swank and *swanky*, adjectives, can be traced to Middle Low German *swank* and Middle Dutch *swanc*, and originally meant supple, active, agile. Robert Burns described his Auld Mare as swank when he meant active, full of herself, and swanky was in use in Scotland as far back as Dunbar's time; he uses the adjective in *Flyting*, published in 1508.

Dunbar, Ramsay in 1715 and Elliot in 1756 show that swanky to them meant strapping, smart, active, and all three used it of young men. Ramsay says that 'The young swankies on the Green / Took round a merry tirle.' Mourning the Scottish dead, Jane Elliot wrote in her great farewell to the young Scots soldiers:

> E'en in the gloaming nae swankies are roaming,
> 'Bout stacks with the lasses at bogle to play:
> But ilk maid sits drearie, lamenting her dearie –
> The Flowers of the Forest are a' wede away.

Can anybody give me information about the grisly little quatrains with a trick last line, known to some as *Little Willies* in honour of the hero of so many of them, and to Americans as *grues*? Robert Hendrickson, the American lexicographer, says that *grue* was coined by Robert Louis Stevenson from *gruesome*. I can find no mention of grue, the verse form, in *Oxford* or in the lesser dictionaries published on this side of the Atlantic. I'd like to know who composed the first one, and if it is true that Stevenson was the first to name the beast. Here's one as I remember it from my schooldays; Hendrickson has a laundered version of it:

> Willie pissed in his oul' lad's tay;
> The oul' lad died, I'm sorry to say.
> His oul' one looked extremely vexed.
> 'For fuck sake, Will,' she said, 'what next!'

Grue in this context must be related to the old word *grue* meaning to feel terror or horror; to shudder, tremble; to shrink from something; to be troubled in heart. The word has a long pedigree. You'll find it in the 1300 *Cursor Mundi*; Barbour uses it in *The Bruce* in 1375, and Holland, *fl.* 1450, was particularly fond of it. Coleridge has the word in the sense 'to thrill': 'His every member grueing with delight.' Grue is neither Anglo-Saxon nor Old Norse, but it does have a Teutonic origin. Compare the Old Swedish *grua*, Old Danish *grue*. It is related to the German *graven* and to the Dutch *gruwen*, to abhor.

I have been asked about gobbledygook by both Helen Jones from Bath and Mary Kennedy from Terence Wogan's home town of Limerick. A newish word, it was coined by an American Congressman, Maury Maverick, in 1944. He was fed up with the jargon of Congressional committees, and wrote a memo that he called *Gobbledygook*. He explained that he coined his word thinking of the noise turkeys made.

Orwell gives a good example of it in his take on Admiral Nelson's 'England expects every man to do his duty': 'England anticipates that, as regards the current emergency, personnel will face up to the issues, and exercise appropriately the functions allocated to their respective occupational groups.' Quite so.

FEBRUARY 2003

WOMEN, IT SEEMS, do not like freckles. Why, I don't understand; I tend towards Dryden's approving view of these little spots in *Palamon*: 'Some sprinkled freckles on his face wre seen, Whose dusk sets off the whiteness of his skin.' A Scottish lady who does not want to be named wrote to me asking where the word came from. She has freckles, she confided, and hates them as much now as she did when she was at school in Durham, where she was called 'freckeldy Scottie' by some of her classmates.

Freckles are spelled *fraclis* in a tract on surgery by Lanfranc, written about 1400. A century and a half later another medical tract gives the intriguing information that *'lac virginis* taketh away freckles of ye visage'. Shakespeare, in a reference to the cowslip in *A Midsummer Night's Dream*, wrote: 'In their gold coats, spots you see, Those be rubies, fairie favours, In those freckles live their savours.'

Freckles, and its rarer singular, are lovely words that evolved from the older English word *frecken(s)*. This is what Chaucer called them in 'The Knight's Tale': 'A few freckness in his face y-spreyned.' The origin of the word is the Old Norse plural *freknur*. Modern Danish has *fregne*.

From Chester came a letter from Henry Hall who used to go *sniggling* for eels when he was young. Some years ago Michael Doorley from Bray, not far from Dublin, asked me about this word. He had heard it in Co. Tipperary and he told me that it meant fishing for eels using a nine-inch hook covered in earthworms. The hook was placed in crevices between rocks in the river, or under bridges. The noun *sniggle*, which means an eel, is found in many of the regional dialects of England. It is found as *snig* in many places as well, and in Cheshire a restless child was said to 'wriggle around like a snig in a bottle'. All over the English Midlands, where they seem to be very fond of snigs, related words emerged, such as *snig-bag*, an eel-bag; *snig-bellied*, said of a very thin animal; and *snig-pie*, an eel-pie. 'A snygge, a ele', is mentioned in a tract dating from 1483, but as to origin, the dictionaries are stuck: 'of obscure origin', I'm sorry to say.

Joseph Wright's great dialect dictionary has the word *spadger* from fourteen counties. I've heard it only once in Ireland, in Cork city, where it is an endearment used of a child, and it's easy to see why: it means a sparrow and, indeed, it is a fanciful alteration of that word. I see that Robinson's *Dialect of Leeds* published in 1862 makes reference to an interesting culinary item, *spadger pie*. Not on many menus nowadays, I'd say.

An interesting word I've heard since coming to live in Dungarvan in southern Ireland is *tack*, meaning pestilence. I was having a drink with a Co. Waterford farmer who used the word with reference to the dreaded foot-and-mouth disease: 'God keep that tack from us,' he said. From the French *tac* this, 'a kind of rot among sheep. Also a plague spot,' according to Randle's Cotgrave's French-English dictionary. The French word is from the Latin *tactus*, found in the sense infectious, contagious disease.

Droll is another word they use in parts of south-eastern Ireland, but not in the sense amusing, eccentric, comical. This droll of theirs is a noun, and I'm told that it exists in England only in the south-west. I've heard it used in Ulster, too. This *droll* means a story. 'If you won't sing us a song,' said an old fellow to me in a Donegal pub, 'give us an oul' droll.' The word is the same as that used of a facial composition, an enacted piece of buffoonery, a puppet show, in use from the mid-17th century but now obsolete. All drolls are adaptions of the French *drole* described by the aforementioned Cotgrave as 'a goodfellow, boon companion, merrie grig, one that cares not which end goes forward or how the world goes'. Pepys has this meaning, too. 'Very merry we were, Sir Thomas Harvey being a merry drole,' he confided to his diary for 7 June 1668.

MARCH 2003

PEOPLE WHO LIVE in our part of the world are never done talking about the weather, and with good reason, I suppose. We are not alone in this; shortly after Christmas I heard Mass in the Cathedral of St Virgil in Salzburg where the priest in his sermon implored his congregation to storm heaven with their prayers for massive falls of snow: their main source of tourist income, of course. I am always glad to get words connected with the weather; one I got recently from Audrey Brown from Nottingham asks about a related subject, the origins of our names for the four seasons.

Let's start with the dreary one we call *winter*, reckoned astronomically from the winter solstice to the vernal equinox – in this part of the world from 22nd December to 20th March. So much for astronomers; the older people where I live in southern Ireland regard All Soul's Day as the start of winter and St Brigid's Day, 1st February, as its end. Brigid was really a fertility goddess, and her feast day is regarded as the first day of spring.

Spenser was right, I think, in simply regarding winter as the frigid time of the year in which a man's breath freezes and sticks to his beard. Winter was also *winter* in Anglo-Saxon, Old Frisian and Old Saxon; Gothic had *wintrus* and *wentrus*, which led some scholars to believe that it came originally from a form of the Indo-European base *-wed*, *-wod*, or *-ud*, reflected in the English words *wet*, *water* and *otter*. 'On sumera hit bith wearm and in wintra ceald,' wrote Aelfred in about 888, stating the obvious.

Spring got its name from the sense that means rising up or springing into existence. In popular use in Britain and Ireland comprising the months of February, March and April; in America, March, April and May. The Anglo-Saxon name for the season was also spring. Spenser described it prettily:

> Lusty Spring is all dight [dressed] in leaves of flowres
> That freshly budded and new bloomes did beare
> In which a thousand birds had built their bowers.

Summer is *sumor* in Anglo-Saxon and *sumer* in Old Norse. A related word outside the Germanic languages is Old Irish *sam*; hence our Modern Irish *samhradh*. The ultimate origin of these words is thought to be the Sanskrit *sama*, season or half-year. Summer is sometimes used to convey the meaning 'year'; witness sentences such as, 'She was a lass of eighteen summers.' Here's old Spenser again:

> Then came the jolly Summer, being deight
> In a thin silken cassock coloured greene,
> That was unlyned all, to be more light ...

That lovely word *autumn* is from Old French *autompne* (modern *automne*), from Latin *autumnus*, a word of uncertain origin. 'Autumpne cometh heue of apples,' sang Chaucer. The term *fall*, used universally in the United States, was once called *the fall of the leaf* in England; indeed fall is still used in some English dialects. In 1545 Roger Ascham had: 'Spring tyme, Somer, faule of the leafe, and winter'. But let Spenser sing us out:

> Then came the Autumne, all in yellow clad,
> As though he joyed in his plentious store,
> Laden with fruits that made him laugh, full glad
> That he had banisht hunger, which to-fore
> Had the belly oft him pinched sore.

Back to the weather, a Common Teutonic word, the Anglo-Saxon being *weder*, the Old Saxon also *weder*, a storm.

Not long ago I heard an interesting word from an old fisherman who lives in these parts. The word is *rag* and it means a sea-fog or a drizzling mist. The word is known in Devon, and in Lancashire and Yorkshire, Joseph Wright's dialect dictionary tells me. Of Scandinavian origin, it appears; the Danish *rag* means a sea-vapour.

The word *sough* is still found in parts of Ireland, Scotland and northern England. It means a murmuring sound such as the sighing or moaning of the wind. Scott had the word in *The Antiquary*: 'Amid the melancholy sough of the whistling wind'. From Anglo-Saxon *swegen*, this lovely word was first used in literature by Chaucer in *The Parliament of Fowles* in 1381.

APRIL 2003

THE WORD *brouhaha*, hubbub, tumult, is used more in the USA than on this side of the Atlantic, as far as I can judge. A man from Penrith, Cornwall, Roger Hempenstall by name, asks where it comes from.

Brouhaha can be traced to a 15th-century French farce in which the Devil made his entrance by shouting 'Brou, brou, ha ha! brou, ha ha!' Not a bad entrance; it must have made his audience sit up and take notice. But where did he get his line? Onomatopoeic, some have said. But Webster's dictionary suggests that the origin of the word may be the Hebrew phrase *barukh habba*, 'blessed be he who enters', from Psalm 118, which has a prominent place in Jewish worship because it is the last of the Hallel psalms, used at the great festivals. The fact that the Italian dialect word *baruccaba* comes from the same phrase and also means hubbub makes the suggestion of a Hebrew origin not all that far-fetched.

I find it strange that brouhaha doesn't appear in English literature until 1890, and even then it was used by an American, Oliver Wendell Holmes, in *Over the Teacups*. He wrote: 'I enjoy the brouhaha of all this quarrelsome menagerie of noise-making machines.'

Shibboleth, a use of language or custom regarded as distinctive of a particular group, also a slogan or catchword used by a particular group, is another word of Hebrew origin. The Hebrew shibboleth was transliterated in the Vulgate as *sciboleth*, and it occurs, *Oxford* says, in the senses 'ear of corn' and 'stream in flood'. The latter fits the bill better than the former, most people agree. The word came into English from an encounter between the victorious Jephthah and the fleeing Ephraimites, described in the book of Judges. The routed Ephraimite stragglers came to a ford on the Jordan held by the enemy. As each man came to the river he was asked to pronounce the Hebrew word for a stream, *shibboleth*. The Ephraimites weren't able to pronounce a *sh* sound and said *sibbolets*, and so, the Good Book tells us, 'There fell at the time of the Ephraimite forty and two thousand.' Quite a brouhaha, you might say. Wyclif, translating Judges in 1382, got the thing arseways: 'They askiden hym, saye thann *sepolech*.' Had he been present on the banks of the Jordan on that fateful day, he would, as they say in Dublin, have had his water cut off.

That good word *stim* has been relegated to dialect status in many dictionaries. It is often spelled and pronounced *styme*. Ronald Gordon of Norwich asks about it. It means the faintest form of any object; a glimpse or gleam of light. 'I scarce could wink or see a styme,' wrote Burns in 'There's Naething Like an Honest Nappy', which is a paean to ale, not to motherhood. Once upon a time an old woman in Co. Donegal, a place that has an ancient affinity with Scotland, told me that a styme was a furtive glance. In an 1828 Scots song book I picked up for half a crown in Edinburgh once, I found the same shade of meaning:

> I see him in aside the bink [bench],
> I gae him bread and ale to drink,
> And ne'er a blythe styme wad he blink.

In Scotland the adjective *stimey* means dim-sighted. Hence the golfing term *stymie*, the predicament in which a player was placed when he found that his opponent's ball lay in the line of his putt. The wicked stymie rule, now gone from the rule book, should be revived. It would give even myself a chance to beat the Tiger. At any rate stime, styme is from the Old Icelandic *skima*, a gleam of light.

Helen Richardson of this parish asked me about the noun *pikey*, a vagrant, tramp, traveller. It is southern English slang. A pikey was a vagrant who used the turnpike roads. Hence the verb *to pike*, to pilfer, and the adjective *pikey*, given to pilfering or petty thefts. *Pike*, as in *turnpike*, was once a fixed barrier on a road to prevent a sudden attack by horsemen; a *turnpike road* was originally a toll-road.

MAY 2003

A FRIEND OF MINE who lives in Co. Down paid me a visit recently and decided to buy a summer house down here by the sea. He is from Yorkshire originally and his speech is adorned with many dialect words and phrases from both places. When I asked him if he missed his native heath he replied, 'I'm not dwining for it, nor am I likely to fall in a dwaum thinking about it.'

To dwine, to decline in health, is common in parts of Ulster, in Scotland and in East Anglia. It survives from Anglo-Saxon *dwinan*, to waste away; there is also the related Old Norse *duina*. It undoubtedly came to the north of Ireland from Scotland with the 17th-century planters; in *Bride of Lammermoor* Sir Walter Scott has 'being up early and down late with his dwining daughter'.

My friend's *dwaum* means a swoon, a fit of weakness. It is in Scots as *dwam*, and is also found as such in northern England, in East Anglia, and in Devon and Cornwall. It is of Teutonic origin; there is the Old Saxon *dwaim*, delusion, and the Anglo-Saxon *dwolma*, chaos.

To barge, to abuse verbally or scold, is a good dialect word common all over Britain and Ireland. John Harte, a Londoner, heard it in southern Ireland recently and tells me that it was one of his mother's words. Where does it come from? he asks.

I don't know, is the honest answer to that question, but I wouldn't discount the theory that it may be a back-formation from *bargee*. These gentlemen were, it would appear, noted for using crude language.

The Irish are rather fond of the word. Sean O'Casey uses it in *The Plough and the Stars*; J.M. Synge has it as well; and Patrick Kennedy, the 19th-century folklorist and storyteller from my own place, described a maiden who 'kep' bargein' an' bangin' him with a beesom'. Good for her; the gorseyjack was acting the maggot, trying his hand, and fondling her and making improper suggestions. A *beesom* is a Wexford brush, by the way.

Now there's a nice one, gorseyjack. It's a word from the fishing village of Kilmore Quay on Wexford's south coast, and nobody under heaven knows what its origin is. When I asked a local chanteuse, Liz Jeffries, to gloss the word for me, she said that a *gorseyjack* was 'a young pup who'd even feel my arse as I walked by him in a pub'. She was a golden oldie at the time, in the early 1970s. God look to her now.

She had another word, fairly common here in the south-east – *baffity*. 'Young ones don't mind being seen in any class of oul' baffity nowadays,' she complained. I also heard a Kilmore gorseyjack speak of a rather large lady: 'She'd take a lot of baffity for a knickers.' Well, *baffity* is a cheap, generally cotton fabric, originally of Oriental manufacture. Is it common in English dialects, I wonder? As to origin, it seems to be from the Persian *baft*, wove.

To call *a spade a spade*. I was recently asked by John Murray, of Old Parish, Dungarvan, Co. Waterford, to say something about the expression's age and origin. He is wrong in thinking that it is no older than the 19th century. It is attributed to Plutarch, who used it in reference to Alexander the Great's father, Philip of Macedon. But the trouble is that there is no evidence that Plutarch used the Greek for 'spade'; the word he used was the one for 'boat'. Erasmus in his Latin translation made a spade *ligo*, confused by the similar Greek words for both spade and boat. Udall's 1542 translation of Erasmus says that the Macedonians, 'altogether grosse, clubbyshe and rusticall ... had not the witte to call a spade by any other name than a spade'. He should have written that they hadn't the wit to call a boat by any other name than a boat. A good example, this, of a mistake in translation giving a language a new and permanent phrase.

JUNE 2003

A MAN WHO has an occasional drink with me in the village in which I now live was talking rugby football. 'He got hurt in the first few minutes of the game,' said he, 'and spent the rest of the game cloppin' about instead of retiring.' The verb *to clop* is not, as you might think from the sound of it, onomatopoeic in origin, but a very old word with a decent pedigree. It means to walk with a limp, and it is found in the south-western counties of England. Its origin is the French *cloper*, to limp, walk lamely, according to Randle Cotgrave's *Dictionarie of the French and English Tongues*, published in 1611.

In Limerick, the word *fear* can mean danger. Speaking about a dangerous shelved beach where hordes of unsupervised children were swimming and playing in the water, a man from that hospitable town recently remarked to me that their parents didn't realize that the youngsters were in such fear. P.W. Joyce, an antiquarian and a Limerickman, wrote in his book, *English as We Speak it in Ireland* (1911): 'Fear is often used among us in the sense of danger.' I mention it here in the hope of finding out if this sense has survived anywhere in England. Did it reach us here in Ireland from some English dialect, I wonder, or did it come directly from the Anglo-Saxon *fær*, peril, sudden calamity? I see that the word is in *Beowulf*: 'Hie se faer begeat ...'

People play cards late into the night in my favourite pub here in Dungarvan-by-the-Sea, and I recently heard a Scotsman exclaim as he led a diamond in a game of 25: 'Diamonds dearly coft for ladies!' The Scots *coft*, which means bought, is an old word, coming from the Middle Dutch *cofte*, past participle of *copen*, to buy. Rhymer Rab has the word in his great *Tam o' Shanter*: 'That sark she coft for her wee Nannie ...' Any trace of the word south of the Scottish border, I wonder? I see that it has reached Ulster, courtesy of the planters of 1609, I suppose.

The great John Ruskin once remarked: 'You must get into the habit of looking intensely at words ... Never let a word escape you that looks suspicious. It is severe work; but you will find it, even at first, interesting, and at last, intensely amusing.' I was suspicious the other day when tending to my one and only rosebush, of a remark of a passing philosopher in relation to his belief that I could get poisoned from a dawk on the stem of my rose. *Dawk*, a prick from a thorn, was, he assured me solemnly, Irish in origin; from *delg/dealg*, thorn, or pin.

'Nay,' quoth I, 'one finds the word *dalk* with the same meaning, a prick from a thorn, in the English counties of Wiltshire, Gloucestershire and Somerset; the Anglo-Saxon is *dalc* and *dolc*; and the Old Norse has *dalkr*, meaning a pin or a clasp, whence the Irish *dealg*.'

'You don't say, now!' he said with ill-concealed disdain, proceeding to the pub where, I heard later, he recounted the conversation we had just had, saying that I was a pathetic bloody West Brit in not admitting that the word was from Irish, and a pretentious old dawk, or some such word, into the bargain.

Gaffer is a common word for an overseer, a foreman; it has now become a soccer player's name for his team's manager. James Turnbull wrote from Wolverhampton about the origin of the word. It was originally applied by country people to an elderly man, and it was a term of respect. In 1742 Joseph Fielding wrote: 'Mr Joseph Andrews was esteemed to be the only son of Gaffer and Gammer Andrews.' Gaffer meaning boss, foreman, wasn't seen in print until 1841, when it was included in a glossary of Shropshire words. Thomas Hardy was one of the first to give the word a slightly disrespectful tone when he wrote, 'I thought it might be some gaffer sent by Government,' in *Tess of the d'Urbervilles*. As to origin, nothing too exciting, I'm afraid: the word is a contraction of *godfather*.

JULY 2003

ALISON BAIRD sent me a good word from Co. Down, Northern Ireland, a word also found in England's North Country, south to Lincolnshire and Nottinghamshire. I haven't come across the word, *gillery*, which means deception, fraud, trickery, in any Scots dictionary, which I find strange because I've heard it myself in Ayr; indeed, an Aberdonian I occasionally have a pint with used it in my presence the other night as we watched a video of Major What's-His-Name trying to con his way to a cool million. At any rate, the *Lincoln Chronicle*, writing about the football hooligans of 1888, said that the game was 'mixed up with the greatest gillery, roguery and blackguardism'. My, how times change.

Gillery is as old as the York Plays of *c*. 1400. It's from the Anglo-French *gillerie*, trickery, from *guiler*, to beguile, deceive, and thus related to the English noun *guile*.

John Parker wrote from Cardiff asking if the word filly, a female foal, is from the Welsh *guil* or *gwil*, a mare. No, although the Scots noun *gillot*, a mare, probably is. *Filly* is from Old Norse *fylja*, a young mare, and it is in English literature since *c*. 1400: there is a reference in the Chester Plays to 'atter and foxe, fillie, mare alsoe'. A filly, meaning a young, lively woman, is at least as old as the Jacobean and Tudor dramatists: Beaumont and Fletcher, in *The Scornful Lady*, first presented on stage in the year of Shakespeare's death, 1616, have: 'A skittish filly will be your fortune, Welford.' To an oldie like me, one of them would surely be the death of me.

That old scoundrel Pepys in his diary for March 1665 uses a vulgar phrase still heard in my neck of the woods; used of a woman, it means to miscarry: 'My Lady Castlemaine is sick again – people think, slipping her filly.' 'Trot filly, trot foal' is an old and a wise adage used by horse breeders, meaning, of course, that a mare or filly will pass on her faults to her offspring. Used of humans as well.

Mrs Mary Duly of Lee-on-the-Solent, Hants, tells me that she recently visited the small village church of Kilpeck in Herefordshire, famous for its many carvings and sculptures, some of them of a very obscene nature, called Sheila-na-gigs in a guidebook to the place. Mary wants to know if there is any link between the word *sheila* here and the word in Australia for a girl, a girlfriend.

Yes. *Sheila-na-gigs* are medieval carvings of women, always nude and represented in the frontal aspect, the legs usually wide apart and the hands so posed as to call attention to the genitalia. They probably echoed some kind of pagan fertility rite. The phrase is Irish – *Síle na gcíoch* – and means 'Sheila of the breasts'. The name Síle, anglicized Sheila, is common in Ireland, indeed in the 18th century *Síle* was a generic name for Ireland in Irish poetry. *Oxford* points out that an early Australian word for a girl is *shaler*, but concedes that it may represent a generic use of the Irish personal name.

To jigget is a good West Country verb, which means to ride a horse at a jog trot; to dandle a child on the knee. Hence the jiggety jog of the nursery rhyme:

> To market, to market, to buy a fat hog
> Home again, home again, jiggety jog.

To jigget also means to gad about, usually said of young women in a distinctly depreciatory tone. That fine 19th-century novelist Elizabeth Gaskell knew all about a contemporary dance called a *jigget*, performed by working men and women and frowned upon by everybody else. 'I ha' learnt the way now,' says a character in *Mary Barton*, a story of life in Manchester, 'two jiggets and a shake.'

Jiggets, and the *jig* it came from, were thought to be from Old French *gigue*, a kind of fiddle. This word, it was said, gave Modern French *gigue*, the dance and dance tune, but it did not; modern *gigue* was simply adopted from English *jig*, an onomatopoeic word with both musical and sexual connotations.

AUGUST 2003

'He's no arrant doing that,' said a man from north Co. Down to a friend of mine recently. My friend correctly identified the word *arrant* as *errand*. He also found the following in a Northern Ireland political journal: 'He is not an elected representative for the area and has no errand to attend the meeting.' Both arrant and errand in this context are found all over Scotland, in northern England and in Shetland. Joseph Wright's great dialect dictionary defined the word as 'business, occupation; figuratively need, call, occasion for'. This was recorded in Cumbria: 'That's what maks him ga rakin about the fell o' neets without an errand.' From Wilson's *Plebeian Politics*, a Scottish tract of 1798, Wright retrieved this: 'Weed'n no arrand for to meddle wi' these French.'

I see that the phrase *once errand*, or *once arrant*, defined by Wright as 'a journey made with a special object in view', still survives in both Scotland and England's North Country. Wright gave this Scots example: 'I'm here, once errand, to ask if you can hear tell of another lass to take her place.' There is another interesting use of errand in W.H. Patterson's glossary of Ulster words published in 1890: 'To make an errand to your face.' He gave an example of the phrase's use: 'Said in anger: If A make an erran' tae yer face it will be no tae kiss ye.' Errand and its variants are from Old English *ærende*, corresponding to Old Norse *eyrinde*, a verbal communication to a third party; an expedition with a specific purpose.

Another old word found in the shadow of the Mourne mountains in Co. Down is *biggin*. This is a hut built by shepherds for a shelter on upland slopes. The word came with the planters from Scotland. Robert Burns wrote of 'Some auld houlet-haunted biggin' in his poem 'On Captain Grose'. Blount's seventeenth-century *Law Dictionary* tells us that 'in the Northern parts it is used for a fair house or gentleman's seat'. The first mention of the word in literature is in the *Cursor Mundi* of about 1300. Origin? The Old Icelandic *bygging*, buildings or houses.

A lady from Henley, who does not want me to disclose her identity, asks if it is true that the phrase *once burned, twice shy* may not be 'as innocent as it sounds'. True enough, dear lady. *Burned* is as old as Shakespeare's time at least, and for centuries it meant infected with venereal disease. You may remember the pun in *King Lear*: 'No heretics burned, but wenches' suitors.' Eric Partridge points us to a memorable definition of *burned/burnt* in the *Dictionary of the Canting Crew* (c. 1690): 'Poxt, or swingingly Clapt'. I have a feeling that *once bitten, twice shy* is a laundered version of the phrase.

I was asked recently by a Dublinman about a word I never heard or saw in print in my life: *lagnours*. I have tried all the usual sources, and I now ask my *Oldie* readers for their help. My friend sent me a photograph of his grandfather's general store-cum-hotel, dating from the 1920s, he thinks, and emblazoned over the door are the words 'Only The Finest Lagnours Supplied'. Can anybody tell him, and me, what lagnours are? I notice that Lagnour is a surname found here and there in England. Could it be that somebody of that name manufactured articles that were sold in the Co. Mayo shop, and if so, what the blazes were they?

Holly Purchase from Penzance, Cornwall, asks about the word *palaver*. She wonders if it is Romany in origin. Nope. The Greek word for what we know as a parable was *parabole*, meaning 'a placing side by side', a comparison. The parables of the Bible were comparisons, in the form of allegorical stories. Now the Greek word came into Latin as *parabola*; the Portuguese borrowed it as *palavra*, and took it with them to Africa in the 16th century, where they extended its meaning: henceforth it meant the long chats they had with the African chiefs they did business with. The English picked up the Portuguese word in Africa in the 18th century, and they called it palaver. A good word.

SEPTEMBER 2003

On a recent visit to Pentire in Cornwall, as I was waiting for a taxi outside a restaurant perched on a cliff-top, I was fascinated by the phosphorescent movement of the sea below me. The night was dark, and I had come outside at the suggestion of a couple who sat near me at dinner. He was from Aberdeen and she was from Shetland, and it was she who waxed lyrical about what she called the *mareel* on the sea. It rushed in glowing streaks towards the shore just as the breakers do in daylight in this surfers' paradise, and it was a phenomenon I had never seen before.

I had never heard the word mareel either, I need hardly say, and I promised the Shetland girl to look it up for her, just to see where it originated. Good old Joseph Wright has it in his monumental dialect dictionary published at Oxford in the early years of the 20th century and now out of print, alas. He quotes Spence's *Folk-Lore* of 1899 in which a Shetlander describes a scene similar to one we saw below us, with the mareel streaking in towards the beach at night with a magical glow, and it came as no surprise to see that the word is Norse in origin, the Danes having *morild* for the phosphorence of the sea, and the Norwegians *moreld*: both from the Old Norse *mauru-eldr*, a light from insects or decomposed matter.

In the same lovely Cornwall, as I was attending my granddaughter Lara's Confirmation service, I overheard a young lass of about six summers complain about her little brother: 'Mummy, he's pooching at me again!' The miscreant was duly reprimanded, and of course, the pooching started again. Often spelled *poach* and *pauch* in the south-western counties, and *potch* in the Midlands, *to pooch* means to poke, especially with the fingers; to thrust, push suddenly; to dig; to prick a hole; and figuratively, to interfere. I knew the word from another context. My native Wexford is famous for its old thatched cottages and I knew *pooch* as a broad wooden instrument used to open an old thatch. The word must have been used in Warwickshire also; In *Coriolanus* Shakespeare has, 'I'll potch at him some way.' The word is from the French *pocher*, to thrust, or dig out with the fingers, according to Shakespeare's contemporary Cotgrave, who gave us a marvellously eccentric French-English dictionary in 1611.

A lovely ceremony it was, and one of the local clergymen complimented the twelve youngsters who were confirmed on being so beautifully pranked. *Pranked* means, I was to find out, decked out, adorned; not in the white dresses of my youth, I might add, but in outfits that would do justice to the fashion houses of London, Paris or Milan. How times change. Pranked is found in dialects from Scotland to Cornwall. It may be related to *prank*, the equivalent of *prance*, with the suggestion of display – this is from *Jack Juggler*, a piece of doggerel from 1560: 'A maid we have at home, Alyson Trip-and-Go. She simpereth, she pranketh and jetteth without fail.'

Roger Proctor wrote from Norwich to ask about place-names that contain the element meals. He knows of places called Branchester Meals and Wells Meals. He can't find this *meal* in the dictionaries he's consulted. You'll find this word, sometimes spelled *meels*, *mels*, or *miels*, in the Lake District, Lancashire, Cheshire, Lincolnshire and East Anglia. It means a sandhill or sandbank. You'll also find compounds such as *meal-bank*, a sandhill or bank of sand blown up by the wind, and *meal-marsh*, low sandy land reclaimed from the sea. The word is, like mareel, of Norse origin. There is the Norwegian dialect word *mel*, a sandbank along a lake or river-course; this, like the Norfolk *meel*, is from Old Norse *melr*, a sandhill overgrown with bent grass. Old Norse also has *mel-bakki*, a sandbank.

OCTOBER 2003

HARRY WILLIAMSON of Ashley Park, Bangor, wrote to me recently about the phrase *stoney-broke* or *stone-broke*, financially ruined. I am not sure where this Bangor is: it could be the one near Belfast or it could be the one in Wales. *Oxford* has nothing to say about the phrase's origin except to describe it as slang; Eric Partridge says that it was in speech before 1887. R.C. Lehmann in *Harry Fludyer* (1890) has this: 'Pat said he was stoney or broke or something but he gave me a sov.' My correspondent, who, like myself, has accepted Partridge's view that it is slang of unknown origin, sent me a copy of the *British National Trust Magazine* of 2002, which, in its 'Hourglass' column, has an interesting tale to tell.

In Gibside House, near Gateshead, there lived in the late 18th century the Countess Mary Eleanor Bowes, known as 'the unhappy countess'. She was an ancestor of the late Queen Mother, had a disastrous taste in men, and was partial to bouts of unbridled *houghmagandie*, Rab Burns's memorable word for what Dubliners call *how's your granny for slack?*, otherwise, fornication. Very wealthy, she attracted a variety of fortune hunters. First she married John Lyon, Earl of Strathmore, a wastrel who went abroad and conveniently died of consumption, while she stayed at home and got pregnant by a rogue called John Grey. Just as Mr Grey was about to do the decent thing by her, urged to do so by outraged letters in the *Morning Post*, along came Andrew Robert Stoney, an impoverished Irish adventurer, who, the article says, gave us the term stoney-broke.

He swept the countess off her feet and into bed, advising her to forget Grey and to marry himself instead. She agreed, they were married, and only then did he discover that she had prudently tied up all her money in a trust fund. Stoney, who came from the village of Borrisokane, Co. Tipperary, forced poor Bowes to write her *Confession*, giving details of her life between the sheets; so she fled him and began divorce proceedings. He followed her, abducted her from her coach and gave her the option of dropping her divorce suit or being shot on the spot. And then, guess what? Out of the morning mist came her friend on horseback and rescued her. They imprisoned the vile Tipperary man, who was convicted and jailed for his sins. He died as he had lived, stoney-broke.

Is this the origin of the slang term, or inspired folk-etymology? I don't know. Anyway, Gibside House is now a ruin, but the National Trust is busy restoring Mary Eleanor Bowes's garden to its original magnificence, perhaps, as the article says, 'cheering the despondent spirit of the unhappy countess'. There you are.

What a merry bunch the followers of Captain Grose, who gave us the great *Dictionary of the Vulgar Tongue*, or the *Lexicon Balatronicum*, were. In 1811 they considerably enlarged Grose's work: they gave their names as A Member of the Whip Club (a coachman); Hell Fire Dick; James Gordon and William Soames. Their book has been republished in paperback; here is a sampler.

In such a dictionary one expects crudities. *Riding St George* is described as 'the woman uppermost in the amorous congress, that is, the dragon upon St George'. *Ballocks*, we are informed, is also a name given to a parson. The meaning of *to roger* hasn't changed, 'from the name Roger being frequently given to a bull'. *To screw* was known to Grose, and a female screw was a common prostitute. *Basket-making* was a term for copulation, indulged in by *bats*, 'low whores, from the practice of moving out at dusk'. James Joyce's Dublin slang for night, *darkmans*, is here; *bene darkmans* was a cant term for 'goodnight'.

There are many words here for a hanging. *The Sheriff's Ball* is one: 'to dance at the Sheriff's Ball and loll out one's tongue at the company' – to be hanged. There are a few good Irish terms here. *Grapple the rails* is one – it means whiskey.

I was pleasantly surprised by the many slang and cant expressions used by England's poor in the late 18th and early 19th centuries that have survived to this day. Surprise yourself by buying this famous book, published by Senate of London, and, as they say, available in all good bookshops.

NOVEMBER 2003

YOU MAY REMEMBER G.M. Hopkins's poem 'Pied Beauty', in which he praises God for dappled things, including 'all trades, their gear and tackle and trim'. Well, the poem suggested to a reader that I put together a little glossary of the tools of all the trades and crafts I can think of, from the miller's to the thatcher's; from the surgeon's to the farrier's; from the baker's to the plasterer's; from the sailmaker's to the knacker's. Should any of my readers have material that would be of assistance to me, may they rest assured that all contributions would be acknowledged, and any books or booklets lent to me returned safe and sound. Thanks to Lawrence Duttson of London for milling words associated with Sturminster Newton Mill. We're off!

Langle is a farmer's word from Scotland, northern England and Ulster. It means a tether connecting a horse's or a cow's two forelegs; there is also a *side-langle* connecting a foreleg and a hindleg. *Langle* used as a verb means to hobble and, figuratively, to tie down: 'She has him well langled,' is an expression I heard used of a newly married man in Seamus Heaney's country, and 'to get out of the langle' is an Ulster way of saying to escape from the wife and go on a spree with the boys for a night.

The word's ultimate origin is disputed. It may be from an unattested Old French *langle*, from Latin *lingula*, a thong, or it may be of Scandinavian origin. Macafee's *Concise Ulster Dictionary* suggests that we consider the Norwegian dialect *langhelda*, literally, 'long hold'. Anyway, thanks to Mrs Anne Maguire for that.

G.H. Rogers has been reading Macaulay's *History of England*. In it he came across: 'A great crowd of squires after a revel, at which doubtless neither October nor claret has been spared.'

This particular *October* was in common use in the 18th century. Steele was, it seems, the first to use it in print, in the *Tatler* in 1709: 'Hours he spent swilling himself with October.' This was simply ale brewed in October, but why this particular month was selected for the brewing I don't know. Can any of my readers help?

Rosalind Gaul from Notting Hill wrote to ask about the word *delicatessen*. Well, the word is in English since the end of the 19th century, and it then meant 'delicacies'. Delicatessen was to Max Beerbohm, say, a plural noun, reflecting its origin in the German *delikatessen*, plural of *delikatesse*. But Max would also have known the word as a singular noun, the shop in which delicacies were sold. The Germans had borrowed the word from the French *délicatesse*, delicacy, the origin of which was probably Old Italian *delicatezza*, delicate, tasty, dainty, from the Latin *delicatus*, pleasing to the senses, voluptuous.

Miss Gaul runs an excellent delicatessen herself, and I must rid her of the widespread notion, often, alas, given credence in some dictionaries, that the word is related to the German verb *essen*, to eat. It ain't.

Dream is a lovely word; June Price of Scarborough asks about it. In Anglo-Saxon it meant either joy, or music, or noise; by the 13th century the word, by then *drem* and *dreem*, had come to mean a series of thoughts, images or emotions occurring during sleep. Why the extraordinary change in meaning? Well, the new meaning was, without doubt, influenced by the Scandinavians, who introduced us to *draumr*, a dream during sleep, a word no doubt related to the Anglo-Saxon word, and to Old High German *troum*, dream. It is also related to the Greek *thrylos*, noise, and to Latvian *dunduris*, a wasp. Consider the Anglo-Saxon meaning of dream – noise. Sweet dreams always!

DECEMBER 2003

I OFTEN WISH I had been taught something about birds in school. I am constantly shamed by my five-year-old granddaughter who knows more about them than I do. One of her new tricks for avoiding going to bed at night is to watch through a night-scope I had bought for her father the deer and foxes that glide through his fields; she also observes some owls that fly from a disused shed. All this is our secret, of course, or so she thinks. She keeps asking me about rarer birds she has seen on television; she can scarcely believe that I can't take her to an osprey nest – me, who wouldn't know an osprey if it alighted on my shoulder.

She isn't interested in words yet, needless to say, but the word osprey is interesting to harmless old drudges like me. David Attenborough has revealed to young Mary that this big fish-eating hawk has evolved many features to help it catch its prey, notably hundreds of spiny things on its feet that make it easy for it to hold slippery fish. I was surprised to find that the word *osprey* came not from any fishy source but from the Latin *ossifraga*, 'bone-breaker', from *ossi*, bone, and *frangere*, to break. Funny, that, because the osprey eats its prey whole and is not noted for breaking bones. What happened is that there was a literary mix-up once upon a time that saddled the osprey with its inappropriate name.

Pliny was the first to use the word ossifraga. You may remember that he was a fine naturalist who went to his reward observing the out-of-control Vesuvius in 79 AD. *Ossifraga*, he said in his *Natural History*, was 'another type of eagle'. Why the French, and later the English, came to the conclusion that Pliny's bird was the osprey nobody knows. Ossifraga became *osfraie* in Middle French, and in Middle English this had become *ospray*.

So, if Pliny's ossifraga wasn't our osprey, what was it? It is now thought that the bone-crusher he had in mind was the lammergeier, a big vulture rather like an eagle, found in parts of Asia and Europe. *Lammergeier* is German for 'lamb vulture' because shepherds blamed it for swooping down on their flocks and carrying lambs away with them. The shepherds were wrong here. The lammergeier doesn't kill lambs, it confines itself to eating carrion, and has a special fondness for bones. Although it is a big bird, with a wingspan of up to ten feet, it has a delicate bill totally unsuited to breaking bones. It solves its problem by taking its bones high up in the air and dropping them onto the rocks below. It is known to drop things other than bones, and the big bird that dropped a dead tortoise from high up on to the bald head of the great Greek dramatist Aeschylus, mistaking it for a rock, was, it is believed, a lammergeier.

It is curious how many words develop a sense so very far removed from their original meaning. Take *amuse*. This verb started life in English meaning to deceive, to cheat, and held that meaning until the end of the 18th century, when it began to take on the meaning 'to entertain'. It came to us from Middle French *amuser*, 'to dilly-dally, to waste time', from Old French, from *a* (from Latin *ad*) plus *muser*, to muse. *Beguile* is another word that once had the same negative meaning as amuse (it survives in *guile*); it now has the meaning 'to entertain, to charm'. Consider the adjective *beguiling* in such a phrase as 'a beguiling person'; it once would have meant a time-wasting, deceiving cheat. And how did *divert*, ultimately from Latin *divertere*, 'to turn away', change its meaning from 'deviate, deflect', to become, in its adjectival form, 'entertaining, amusing'? And how did all three words end up with the new sense of 'entertain'? Webster's charming, diverting and entertaining *Word Histories* suggests that in all three instances the evolution of the new sense 'entertain' arose from the images of leading someone away from his or her cares.

I wish you a Christmas free of care. *Go mbeirimid beo ar an am seo arís* – may we all be alive at this time next year.

JANUARY 2004

A HAPPY NEW YEAR to you all. From now on, the old 'uns say, we can look forward to longer days, and, in Ireland at least, to the coming of spring on 1st February, the feast of St Brigid. The great Joseph Wright, in his monumental *English Dialect Dictionary*, gives this from Gloucester: 'From Christmas-tide to New 'us-tide the days do get a cock's stride.' The notion is not confined to England. W.H. Patterson has: 'About oul' New Year's Day, the days is a cock-stride longer.' Hogg, the bard of Selkirk, referred to the New Year cockstride in 1822. A cheering thought in these short, gloomy days.

A letter from Jane Osborne in Norfolk reminds me that when I was young it was customary for some of us to ply young ladies with Liebfraumilch 'to coax their motions in high degree', as a 19th-century broadside ballad so delicately put it. It never worked, in case you're interested. *Liebfraumilch*, which may be rendered the milk of the lovely or gentle woman, is, I was told by a Munich waiter recently, what most American tourists ask for, regarding it as the archetypal German wine. It is not, I venture to say, one of the world's great wines; as a matter of fact most of it is bloody awful, but the history of the name is interesting. In the city of Worms, famous as the site of the Concordat of 1122 and the Diet of 1521, stands the lovely Gothic church called *Liebfrauen-kirche*, which has a vineyard known as the *Liebfrauenstift*, which once produced the wine called Liebfraumilch. *Stift* may be rendered endowment; giving us the clue that the church and its vineyard were once upon a time endowed by some noble gent. The *liebfrau* is, of course, the Madonna, *milch* is milk. The name is lovely, and let's not be too harsh on the original wine from the Worms vineyard.

Unscrupulous growers along the Rhine, especially those of the Rheinhessen, a district south and west of Mainz, began to call their poorest wines Liebfraumilch too, and in 1971 the Germans gave the Rheinhessen vineyards permission to retain the name Liebfraumilch, on condition that the stuff in the bottles be 'pleasant to drink'. The old vineyard at Worms retaliated by calling their wine *Liebfrauenstiftswein*. It is not bad at all but, it seems, too big a mouthful for American tourists, who buy by the label.

Ostracize and *ostracism* first appeared in English in the 16th century. In those days the schoolmasters imparted a very good grounding in the classics to their pupils and these two words were used at the time to refer to an Athenian custom. The figurative use of these words is now common, of course, and social ostracism, exclusion from acceptance by a class or group, makes the news frequently. John Donne, by the way, was the first to use *ostracism* in the figurative sense, in a letter to the Duchess of Bedford: 'I have been told, that vertue in courtiers hearts / Suffers an Ostracisme, and departs.' But the schoolmasters of Master Shakespeare's day would have known that the Greek word *ostrakon*, a shell, or an earthenware vessel, or a shard of such a vessel, was related to *ostreon*, oyster, and *osteon*, bone, and that these Greek words name brittle things. In Athens these broken earthenware fragments were put to good use. Once a year the populace would come together in the *agora* or marketplace and vote to banish keo-boys, and other types considered dangerous, from the city. The names of those deemed fit for temporary expulsion were written on an *ostrakon*, and if at least 6000 people voted, the man who got the most votes was ostracized, and given his marching orders. Dorothy Birmingham from Croydon asked.

Helen Trench from Luton wrote about wimp. This is one of those slang words born out of the light, as somebody said, and we can only guess as to its origin. My own guess is that it's from another slang *wimp*, a girl, a waif, a word found in the old London glossaries.

FEBRUARY 2004

I HAVE BEEN ASKED by an erudite reader from Attleborough, Norfolk, Joan Richardson by name, why some of the great dictionaries don't agree about the etymology of the word jinx. *Oxford*, my correspondent points out, doesn't even attempt a guess, and rightly so, in my view, because the evidence is confusing, as we'll see; H.L. Mencken, the American lexicographer, agreed. Eric Partridge thought that the word's origin is the Scots *jink*, 'to make a sudden turn'; we hear the word often from rugby commentators, used as an adjective in phrases such as 'a jinking run'. But jinking runs, as from those two masters of the craft, Mr Robinson of England and Mr Hickie of Ireland, don't put a jinx on games, so I think we should discount Partridge's theory. *Oxford* points out that the word *jinx*, noun and verb, was first seen in print in American books and newspapers dealing with baseball, but it jumps to no conclusions from that fact. Among the first to use the word was a man called Christy Mathewson, a famous player in his day, who wrote in *Pitching in a Pinch*, published in 1912: 'A jinx is something which brings bad luck to a ballplayer.'

Take note that Webster, the *Random House Dictionary*, and Hendrickson's *Encyclopedia of Words and Phrases* have an interesting theory as to the word's origin. Back in the dark ages, there lived a bird called the *jynx* which, it was believed, used to put spells on people. This bird took its name from its Greek name, *iynx*. It had an ugly, twisted neck, strange feeding and breeding habits, and only let its strident cries be heard as it prepared for migration. The rest of the time it maintained a complete silence, and this, it is thought, gave the populace the notion that it might be a favourite of the powers of darkness. And so they made love potions of the jynx's feathers, and the bird's name was soon given to any black magic charm or spell used on a selected victim. All that evidence seems enough to suggest that the slang term jinx originated in jynx, but, as Hendrickson says, the long flight of the jynx from medieval times to the printed pages of the baseball books of the early 20th century is not easily explained. *Oxford*, I think, is correct in not giving Webster's attractive theory its blessing. The jynx is known in America, by the way, as the wrynecked woodpecker, often shortened to wryneck.

Job is an interesting word, and it is not slang, as is often thought. In the sense of *Oxford*'s first definition, 'a piece of work, especially a small piece of work done in the way of one's own special occupation or profession', it is first found in literature in 1627, in Middleton's *Mayor Quinborough*: 'I cannot read. I keep a Clark to do those small jobs for need.' Jonathan Swift, who was as cantankerous about the use of slang as he was about most things, used the word in his correspondence and gave it his approval by doing so: 'I am strongly tempted to send a parcel to be printed ... and make a ninepenny job for the bookseller.' A *job*, meaning a theft, robbery or other illicit business, *is* slang, underworld 18th-century slang that has survived. Defoe, in *Moll Flanders* has: 'It was always reckoned a safe job when we heard of a new shop.'

I am sad to tell you that job has become a slang word used in Irish funeral parlours. I entered one a few years ago with a young man who had played prop forward at rugby for his country, to pay our respects to a young woman who had lost her life in a traffic accident. We were a little early, and were greeted by an oaf in black suit and tie who enquired, 'Which job do yiz want to see?' He was lucky he didn't himself end up in a coffin, as my companion was a close friend of the deceased.

Where, then, does the word come from? Some have offered, rather tentatively, the older *job*, a small piece, a lump, a word derived, perhaps, from *gob*, a lump, from Old French *gober*. Where the connection is, I cannot, for the life of me, see. Best say that it is of uncertain origin, I think.

MARCH 2004

A YOUNG FRIEND of mine who has been reading the adventures of Marco Polo asked me if we can believe anything your man said about the mysterious East when he could write this about the unicorn: 'It is a hideous beast, and not at all like what we think and say it is in our countries.' Marco was used to the depictions of the unicorn in European painting, and thought he knew what a unicorn should look like: a dainty, horse-like animal, pure white in colour, with a long tapering horn protruding from its forehead. The unicorn was a revered image, and in the works of European writers its capture and death became a symbol of the death of

Christ. The graceful animal we see on medieval tapestries is based on a real animal that disappointed the Venetian traveller.

What Marco Polo saw was an animal first described by the Greek traveller Ctesias in the 4th century BC, the Indian rhinoceros, and called 'the Indian wild ass' by him. It had, Ctesias wrote, a white body, a dark red face and dark blue eyes, and had a horn protruding from its face that was of great value as an aphrodisiac and as a cure for epilepsy. Now Ctesias was never in India; he relied on the writings of other travellers to that land for information on his 'wild ass'. The massive, ungainly animal was eventually given the name *rhinoceros*, from the Greek words *rhin-* 'nose', and *keras*, 'horn'. The African rhino, with its two horns, was unknown to the Greeks.

As for *unicorn*, this is how the word entered English. In the 3rd century BC the translators of the Old Testament from Hebrew into Greek had a problem with a beast they found in the book of Job. This creature was called *re'em*, and it is now thought that it was the extinct aurochs or wild ox. The ancient Greek scholars, mistaking it for Ctesias's beast, settled on the name *monokeros*, one horn. The Latin version of the Bible made *unicornus* of the Greek word, from Latin *uni*, one, and *cornu*, horn, and the King James Bible made unicorn of it in English. And so the folklore and other vague notions of two animals, the Indian rhino and the aurochs, were conflated to give the medieval word for the imaginary animal that may be seen skipping over the landscape in the old tapestries.

I don't know of any writer who made a symbol of any kind of rhinoceros, but I do know that G.K. Menzies, born in 1869, wrote a very funny poem in a Scots dialect when he read in the South African press that 'Two men were fined £120 apiece for poaching a white rhinoceros.' He called his verse 'Poaching in Excelsis'.

> I've poached a pickle paitricks [a few partridges] when the leaves were turnin' sere,
> I've poached a twa-three hares an' grouse, an' mebbe whiles a deer,

But ou, it seems an unco [strange] thing, an' jist a wee mysterious,
Hoo any mortal could contrive tae poach a rhinocerious.
I've crackit [gossiped] wi' the keeper, pockets packed wi' pheasants' eggs,
An' a ten-pun' saumon hangin' doun in baith my trouser legs,
But eh, I doots effects would be a wee thing deleterious
Gin [if] ye shuld stow intil yer breeks a brace o' rhinocerious.

I mind how me an' Wullie shot a Royal in Braemar,
An' brocht him doun tae Athol by the licht o' mune an' star.
An' eh, Sirs! but the canny beast contrived tae fash [trouble, annoy] an' weary us –
Yet stags maun be but bairn's play beside a rhinocerious.

I thocht I kent o' [knew about] poachin' jist as muckle's [as much as] ither men,
But there is still a twa-three things I doot I dinna ken;
An' noo I cannot rest, my brain's growin' that deleerious
Tae win awa to Africa an' poach a rhinocerious.

APRIL 2004

JAMES HENNESSY, from Dublin's charming little seaside town, Dalkey, who has been reading 18th-century sermons, for amusement, he says, and not for edification, wrote to ask about two words he noted down, Phryne and hetaira. The number of times these words were used by the ranting preachers of the day suggested that they were aimed at practitioners of what Rab Burns called *houghmagandie*, fornication, or what Dubliners call *a rub of the relic*.

Hetairai were first described in literature by Herodotus. Despite modern and ancient arguments to the contrary, hetairai is simply the Attic euphemism for those women, slave or free, who traded their sexual favours for long or short periods outside wedlock, whether they were streetwalkers, the inmates of civic or private brothels, or accomplished or expensive courtesans. The *Oxford Classical Dictionary* says that they were tolerated until the coming of Christianity because of the social protection they offered as an alternative to adultery; they enjoyed legal status in most cities. They were often accused of being socially dangerous because of their rapacity and the ruinous infatuation they could inspire in the young; some of the greatest oldies of ancient Greece patronized them, however, and a literature grew, telling of hetairai with hearts of gold and of well-bred hetairai forced to ply their trade reluctantly by cruel stepfathers or ne'er-do-well husbands. The most famous of them were Lais, Neaera, Thais and my correspondent's Phryne.

What a woman Phryne was, this Athenian beauty who achieved fame and fortune and immortality in the 4th century BC. She became so rich that she could offer to rebuild the walls of Thebes

if the inscription 'Destroyed by Alexander, restored by Phryne the hetaira' was cut into the stone over the city's main gate. Her generous offer was rejected, I'm sorry to say. She was one of the greatest beauties of all time, but she fell foul of a kind of puritanism that was affecting Athens at the time, and was charged with gross indecency or impurity, a capital crime under the new laws. She was defended by one of her lovers, the great orator Hyperides. He pulled off one of the most famous courtroom stunts of all time when, as things looked very bleak indeed for her, he walked across to where she stood and ripped off her dress. 'You look', he said to the judges, 'on Greece's greatest beauty. Is she not a child of the gods? What god would not desire her? What god would call her a whore? Look well on her, and then consider your verdict.' She walked free on the arm of Hyperides, to tumultuous applause.

The word *courtesan* was borrowed into English from the Old French *courtisane*, from the Italian *cortigiana*, literally woman of the court, from *corte*, court, from Latin *cohort*. It originally meant a person, male or female, attached to the court of a prince; later it came to mean a high-class prostitute. *Concubine*, a kept mistress, arrived in English from Old French before 1300. The French had *concubine*, from Latin *concubina*, from *con*, together + *cubare*, to lie. The pre-1300 *Cursor Mundi* tells us that 'O quens had [Solomon] hundrets seven; Thre hundrets concubins'; they must have kept him in shape. Chaucer in *The Canterbury Tales* tells of a boozer who 'wolde suffer for a quart of wine A goode felawe to han his concubyn A twelve moneth.'

The word *harlot* originally meant a male fornicator. It was a borrowing from Old French *herlot*, and was related to Italian *arlotto*, a glutton. The ultimate history of this widely diffused Romantic word is unknown. It came to mean a female prostitute by 1485, and in 1570 it was suggested that it was derived from the name of William the Conqueror's mother, Arlette or Herleva. This was widely believed.

I was shocked, gentle reader, to find some dictionaries describing the beautiful Phryne as a harlot. A hetaira she was proud to call herself. I'll drink to that.

MAY 2004

READERS of this column must know by now that I have a tolerance for people who take educated guesses as to the origin of words, no matter how far off the mark these guesses turn out to be. Now an erudite oldie from Norfolk, a university friend of mine from auld lang syne, phoned me recently to remind me of a rare word we both remembered from our youth in Co. Wexford, fewterer, and to tell me that she had found its origin after a long search. *Fewterer* is an old term for a dog-keeper, and my friend heard it used in Norfolk of a man who, like Don Quixote, once kept greyhounds for coursing. Bailey's 18th-century dictionary defined the word as both a dog-keeper and the man who lets greyhounds loose in the chase, a *slipper* I think the modern term is.

Now my friend figured out that the word is connected with the Old English *feute*, the scent or trace of a hare, fox, or deer. She didn't get this notion of hers from the wind, of course, but from the medieval glossary *Promptorium Parvulorum Sive Clericorum*, which has *fewte*, from the Latin *vestigium*, a trace, track, it claimed. Another old tract, *William of Palerne*, has, my friend tells me, 'He fond [found] the feute al freshe.'

Ah dear, it broke my heart to tell such an old friend that her claim is a classic example of folk etymology – erudite but, alas, false. The Middle English *vewter* and the early Modern English *fewterer* are corrupted adoptions of Anglo-French *ventrier*, found in Anglo-Latin as *veltrarius* in the same sense, dog-keeper. The Anglo-French word is from the Old French *veutre, vautre, veltre*, from popular Latin *veltrum*, from Latin *vertragus*, a greyhound. This last is a Gaulish word, from Celtic *ver*, intensive prefix, and the root *trag*, to run. *Sir Gawain and the Green Knight* had *vewter* in 1340; Blount's *Law*

Dictionary has *vautrier*, 'hence our corrupted word *feuterer*, a dog-keeper'.

Another group of words, more common that fewterer, have been exercising the minds of lexicographers for many years. These are the compounds that have life as a first element: life-buoy, life-guard, life-belt. It used to be taken for granted that the *life* part in these compounds meant existence, but that is now thought to be folk etymology.

Life-belt probably means etymologically a body-belt, *life-guard* a body-guard, and *life-buoy* a body-buoy: from the Dutch *lijf*, corresponding to Swedish *lif*, German *Leib*, the body. Think of the old-fashioned German words *Leibbinde*, a girdle; *Leibgurtel*, a body belt; Dutch *lyf-band*, a sash or girdle; Swedish *lif-rock*, a close-fitting coat. Formations similar to life-guard, i.e. body-guard, are the Swedish *lif-vakt*, and the German *Leibgarde*, body-guard.

All right. Let's now concentrate on a word sent to me by Ivan Levey, who wrote from New Cut Rigg, Edinburgh. On a Lancashire bus he recently overheard a mother saying to her teenaged daughter who sat opposite her, 'Jean, you're showing your trolleys.' Mr Levey's Lancashire wife told him that *trolleys* were knickers. 'It gives a whole new meaning to the supermarket sign, "No trolleys beyond this point",' he observes.

As to the origin of the word, Eric Partridge points to *trollywags*, trousers, in vogue around 1870, rhyming slang based on *bags*, pants. The Lancastrians simply used the first element for knickers. But where did this *trolly* come from? I phoned my Norfolk friend. From the obsolete verb *to troll*, to entice, allure, attested to by *Oxford*, she suggested – composing another folk etymology, I'd say – 'what Jean was up to on the bus'. She scorned my proposal that *troll* is a figurative and jocose meaning of the verb *to troll*, to drag along the ground. 'Do you know anything at all about Lancashire girls' knickers?' she asked. 'Miss Lewinsky's were like parachutes compared to them.' Now how the hell would I know?